PUZZLE SQUARE

BRAIN TWISTERS

PUZZLE SQUARE

BRAIN TWISTERS

INCLUDING SUDOKU, NUMBER GRIDS, LOGIC PATHS, AND BATTLESHIPS

LUKE HALL

THUNDER BAY
P · R · E · S · S
San Diego, California

Thunder Bay Press
An imprint of the Advantage Publishers Group
5880 Oberlin Drive, San Diego, CA 92121-4794
www.thunderbaybooks.com

ISBN 13: 978-1-59223-613-8
ISBN 10: 1-59223-613-8

Printed in Singapore.

1 2 3 4 5 10 09 08 07 06

INTRODUCTION

Puzzling is one of life's great pleasures as well as one of the oldest. Did you know that puzzles have been around as far back as the days when Ur and Babylon were major powers in the world?

Yes, the urge to set and solve problems goes right back to the dawn of civilization, and when you are doing puzzles you are part of an ancient and honorable tradition of mental gymnastics.

Research has shown that people who solve puzzles are more likely to remain bright, alert, and in good mental shape longer because they have chosen to engage in this fascinating and stimulating hobby.

And we have chosen a fascinating selection, suitable for everyone from beginners to past masters, to keep you on your toes. The choice includes picture puzzles—from find the hidden object to spot the differences; word puzzles—from anagrams to symbol challenges; number puzzles—from number crosswords to network number connections; and logic puzzles—from classic logic to color sequence puzzles.

You'll discover that puzzling is not only good for you but highly enjoyable as well. So turn the page, kick back, and have fun with the 400-plus puzzles that we have selected for you.

1 · PILE UP

These piles of blocks aren't the random results of a child playing but clues to a final, at present blank, pile on the right. Like the rest, that one has six blocks each with a different one of the six letters. The numbers below the heaps tell you two things:

(a) The number of adjacent pairs of blocks in that column that also appear adjacent in the final pile.

(b) The number of adjacent pairs of blocks that make a correct pair but the wrong way up.

So:

would score one in the "Correct" row if the final heap had an A directly above a C and one in the "Reversed" row if the final heap had a C on top of an A. From all this, can you create the final pile before it topples?

| Correct | 0 | 2 | 1 | 0 | 5 |
| Reversed | 1 | 0 | 1 | 0 | 0 |

Answer on page 470

2 · TRILINES

Which three straight lines, drawn between opposing reference numbers, will divide the square into six parts, each containing three different pairs of animals?

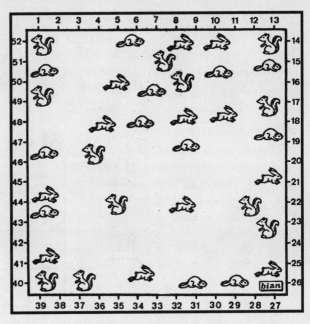

Answer on page 470

Each line, across and down, should contain each of the letters A, B, and C, and two empty squares. The letter outside the grid shows the first or second letter in the direction of the arrow. Can you fill in the grid?

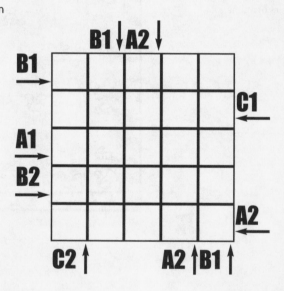

Answer on page 470

4 · SHELF LIFE

Which one of the six drawers should the handyman choose to match the two already in place?

Answer on page 470

5 · SAFE BET

This is an odd type of safe. If you solve all the clues and enter them in the grid, the correct combination will appear in the shaded squares.

ACROSS

1 Subtract 22,289 from 3 across
3 4 percent of 1,111,100
5 Subtract 200 from 6 across
6 Add 4 to 3 down
8 Add 526 to 5 across
10 Square root of 12,321
11 Square first four digits of 25 across
17 Square first four digits of 1 across
19 Half of 6 across
20 Add 13 to 10 across
21 Last three digits of 1 across
23 Add 4 to 21 across
24 Half of 3 across
25 Add 10,416 to 8 across

DOWN

1 Square 23 across
2 Square root of 258,064
3 Square first two digits of 1 across
4 Twice 1 across
5 Add 2,368,131 to 4 down
7 Add 5,783,078 to 5 down
9 Add 370 to 23 across, then multiply by 40
12 Subtract 33 from 15 down
13 Next in series 313, 412, 511, ...
14 Subtract 312 from 3 down
15 Subtract 260 from 22 down
16 Multiply 2 down by 44
18 Add 6 to 3 across
22 Add 4 to 2 down
23 Subtract 10 from 10 across

Answer on page 470

6 · BLOCKS AWAY

The archaeologist has realized that there will be three blocks missing if he tries to reconstruct the original mural shown. Which ones are they?

Answer on page 470

7 · MAZE WAYS

Which route must each numbered ship take to reach its destination of the same number—without crossing the path of any of the other three?

Answer on page 470

8 · BATTLE ZONE

Can you find the detail in each picture that is missing from the other three?

Answer on page 470

9 · ABSTRACTS

Geoff has bought one of the four abstract paintings shown at the top, but he can't remember which one it is or which way up it should go. Can you help him?

Answer on page 470

Two of the pictures are identical, but each of the others differs in one small detail. Which are the "twins," and what are the differences?

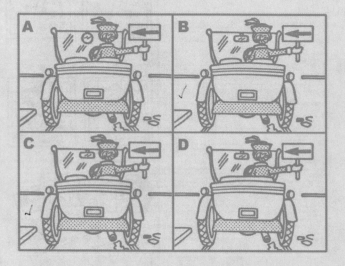

Answer on page 470

11 · IDENTIGRIDS

Which three squares are exactly the same? Be careful—they are not necessarily the same way up!

Answer on page 470

12 · DROPOUT

The collector is trying to select a snail. In the bottom picture, he has made his choice. Which snail did he choose?

Answer on page 470

13 · DEER DEER

Can you spot ten differences between the reindeers' Christmas parties?

Answer on page 470

Help the children and their dog untangle their kites. Follow the lines to see whose kite is whose.

Answer on page 470

Each line, across and down, should contain each of the letters A, B, and C, and two empty squares. The letter outside the grid shows the first or second letter in the direction of the arrow. Can you fill in the grid?

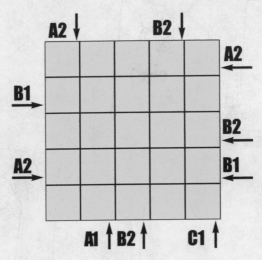

There are eight differences between the two cartoons. Can you spot them?

Answer on page 471

17 · SQUARE PAIRS

In this picture there are six pairs of identical squares.

Can you find them?

Answer on page 471

18 · SUDOKU

Place a number from 1 to 9 in each empty square so that each row, each column, and each 3x3 block contains all the numbers from 1 to 9.

	3			9			6	
6		1	8		5	4		7
	8		3		1		2	
	6	7	5		8	2	1	
5								4
	4	3	2		9	6	7	
	2		9		3		5	
3		9	1		6	8		2
	7			5			9	

Answer on page 471

19 · DROPOUT

The professor is choosing a book. In the bottom picture, he has made his choice. Which one has he bought?

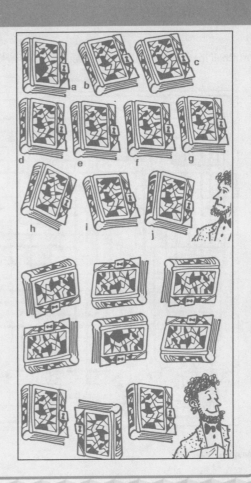

Answer on page 471

20 · WIRED UP

Which of the four plugs should be inserted in the socket to operate the toothbrush?

Answer on page 471

21 · FRAME-UP

Paul took a photograph of his girlfriend in the aviary at the local zoo. Which bird in the aviary is the same as the one in the photograph?

Answer on page 471

22 · DOMINO SEARCH

A standard set of dominoes has been laid out, using numbers instead of dots for clarity. Using a sharp pencil and a keen brain, can you draw in the lines to show where each domino has been placed? You may find the check grid useful—crossing off each domino as you find it.

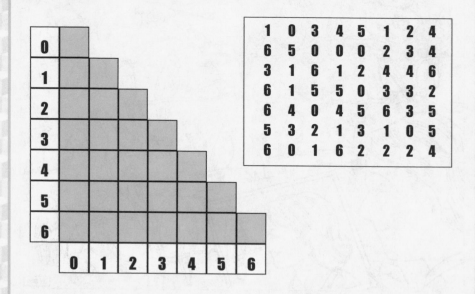

	0	1	2	3	4	5	6
0							
1							
2							
3							
4							
5							
6							

1	0	3	4	5	1	2	4
6	5	0	0	0	2	3	4
3	1	6	1	2	4	4	6
6	1	5	5	0	3	3	2
6	4	0	4	5	6	3	5
5	3	2	1	3	1	0	5
6	0	1	6	2	2	2	4

Answer on page 471

23 · NUMBER JIG

3 figures
178
212
375
575
~~604~~
619
715
830

5588
6048
6543
7142
7891
8106
8341
9012
9867

51279
57267
65432
70000
71847
81736
87653
90103
98314

4 figures
1802
2124
2991
3017
3201
4000
4057
5000

5 figures
13275
14448
15290
21543
37465
43125
45678
45687

6 figures
140747
190668
555855
626206
754321
846684

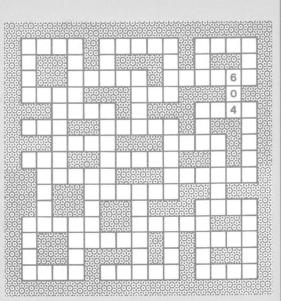

Fit the numbers into the grid as quickly as possible. One has been done for you.

Answer on page 471

24 · DOES IT ALL ADD UP?

The numbers 1–8 have been inserted into the grid so that no two consecutive numbers appear in the same row or column. Any number may appear up to four times. The numbers on the left and above show the totals of the numbers in the row and column respectively. There are no 7s; there is only one 3, which is immediately below a 5; the four center numbers total 18 and are all different; the numbers in the diagonal top right to bottom left total 14. Can you complete the grid?

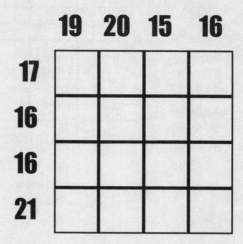

25 · CHINESE I SPY

There are six pairs of identical squares in this picture of the Great Wall of China. Can you spot them?

Answer on page 471

Can you see which five squares of the picture have been reproduced on the right? Watch out—they might not be the same way up!

Answer on page 471

27 · TWISTING TRAILS

Help Farmer Barley reach his sheep and then find his way with his flock to the sheep pen.

Answer on page 471

28 · CARDS ON THE TABLE

The 13 cards of a suit are shuffled and dealt out in a row, and it is found that none is in its correct numerical position (ace left, king right), and the face cards are not at either end or adjacent to each other. The ace is between 9 (left) and 8, 4 between queen (left) and jack, 2 two places left of 10, 7 two places left of 3, the left end card one higher than the right end card, and the king is left of the queen. The ninth and tenth cards from the left total 9, the ninth being of lower value. Can you locate each card?

Answer on page 471

29 · MAZE WAYS

What route should each worker take to get to his or her respective place of work without crossing the path of any of the other three?

Answer on page 472

Can you find the detail missing in each picture that is present in the other three?

Answer on page 472

31 · TWISTING TRAILS

Messy Mandy has mixed up her favorite toys! Follow the lines to sort them out.

Answer on page 472

32 · SUDOKU

Place a number from 1 to 9 in each empty square so that each row, each column, and each 3 x 3 block contain all the numbers from 1 to 9.

		5	6		7	4		
	9		1		2		5	
1			5	8	4			2
6	5	8				1	9	7
		3				5		
9	4	1				6	2	3
5			3	7	1			4
	7		8		9		1	
		6	2		5	8		

Answer on page 472

33 · TRIPLETS

Which three of the waiters are carrying
identical buckets?

Answer on page 472

34 · SAFE BET

This is an odd type of safe. If you solve all the clues and enter them in the grid, the correct combination will appear in the shaded squares.

ACROSS

1   Multiply 29 across by 100, then add 9 across

3   Subtract 2,356 from 21 across

5   Add 10 to 9 across

6   Add 34 to 22 down, then multiply by 3

9   Divide 10 down by 24

11   Square root of 1,022,121

13   Subtract 811 from 3 across

15   Square 1 down

19   Square 3 across

21   Add 1,022 to 22 down

23   Multiply 9 across by 87

25   Add 1 to 5 across

26   Multiply 3 across by 3, then multiply by 10

29   First two digits of 10 down

30   Twice 3 across

31   Subtract 9 from 3 across

DOWN

1   Multiply the last digit of 20 down by 265

2   Add 80 to 3 down

3   Last three digits of 1 down

4   3 percent of 300,600

5   Subtract 30 from 18 down

6   5 percent of 22,839,100

7   Subtract 2,754,362 from 19 across

8   Subtract 34,945 from 6 down

10   Subtract 8,730 from 4 down

12   Add 3 to 9 across, then multiply by 989

14   Add 309 to 6 across

16   Add 459 to 17 down

17   Add 312 to 20 down

18   Subtract 30 across from 24 down

20   First three digits of 12 down

22   Square root of 11,108,889

24   Twice 1 down

27   Add 187 to 28 down

28   Next in series 424, 523, 622 ...

Answer on page 472

Answer on page 472

How many circles are needed to balance scale C?

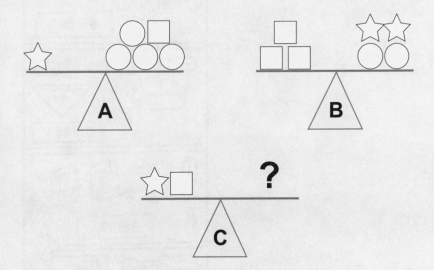

Answer on page 472

37 · SUM-UP

Calculate the price of each screwdriver, hammer, tape measure, and set square.

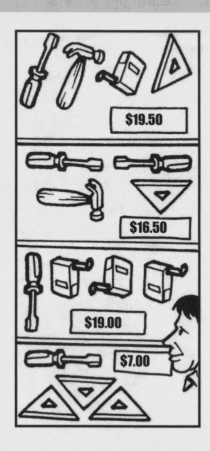

Answer on page 472

38 · SNAPSHOTS

These vacation snapshots are in a muddle!
Can you put them in the right order from the
sun just coming over the horizon, to its highest
point in the sky?

L.AMPITT.

Answer on page 472

39 · DOG TIRED

Each picture is missing a detail that is present in the other seven. Can you spot all eight missing details?

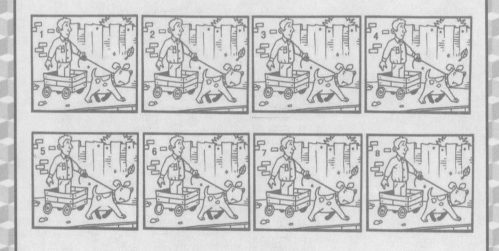

Answer on page 472

40 · NUMBER JIG

Fit the numbers into the grid as quickly as possible. One has been done for you.

2 figures	4 figures	~~81234~~
17	2240	98936
35	3049	
70	3681	**7 figures**
98	4257	6182492
	5326	
3 figures	7502	**9 figures**
147	7987	140311890
279	9366	410637389
386		
623	**5 figures**	
825	19282	
914	24617	
	50109	

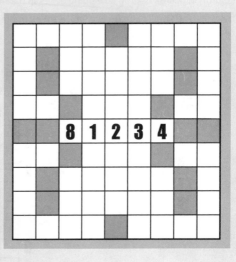

Answer on page 472

41 · LOGI-PATH

Use your deductive reasoning to form a pathway from START to FINISH moving either horizontally or vertically (but not diagonally). The number at the beginning of every row or column indicates exactly how many boxes in that row or column your pathway must pass through. The small diagram is given as an example of how it works.

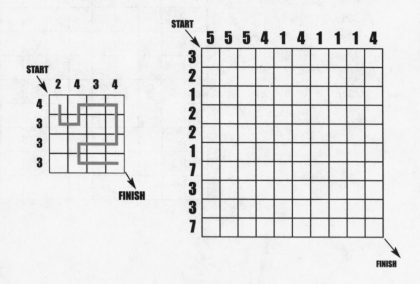

Answer on page 473

42 · ON THE SHELF

The young professor is trying to sort out the shelves in his lab. Can you help him by working out which three objects appear only once?

Answer on page 473

43 · BLACKOUT

Can you see which two dinosaurs are shown in silhouette at the top?

Answer on page 473

44 · BATTLESHIPS

Do you remember the old game of battleships? These puzzles are based on that idea. Your task is to find the vessels in the diagram. Some parts of boats or sea squares have already been filled in, and a number next to a row or column refers to the number of occupied squares in that row or column. The boats may be positioned horizontally or vertically, but no two boats or parts of boats are in adjacent squares—horizontally, vertically, or diagonally.

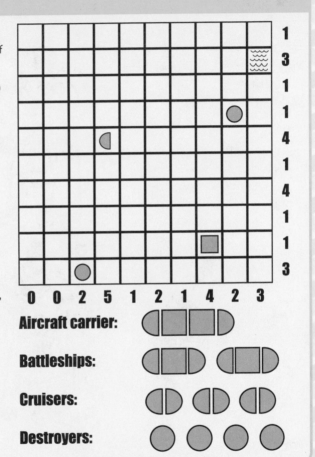

Aircraft carrier:

Battleships:

Cruisers:

Destroyers:

Answer on page 473

45 · TOGA PARTY

Each picture contains a detail that is not in the other three. Can you spot the four extra details?

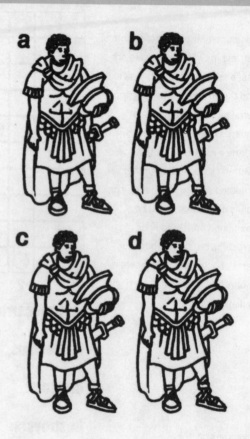

Answer on page 473

Four of the harp players have mirror images. Which are the four pairs and which is the odd one out?

Answer on page 473

The shapes below all appear in the picture somewhere, although they may have been rotated or flipped over. Can you spot them?

Answer on page 473

Place a number from 1 to 9 in each empty square so that each row, each column, and each 3 x 3 block contain all the numbers from 1 to 9.

			7		2			
		2	4	9	3	6		
	9	3	8		1	4	5	
6	3	4				9	7	1
	1						3	
9	5	8				2	4	6
	2	5	6		4	1	8	
		6	3	1	9	7		
			2		5			

Answer on page 473

How many circles are needed to balance C?

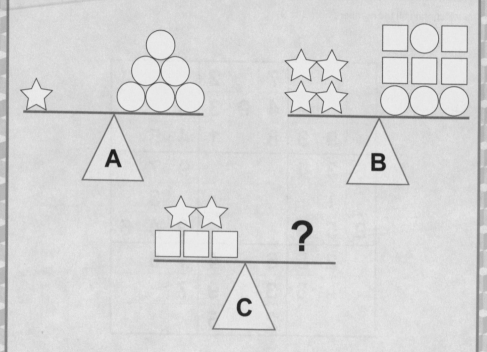

Answer on page 473

50 · BLOCKS AWAY

The professor has discovered that there will be three blocks missing if he tries to reconstruct the original mural shown. Which ones are they?

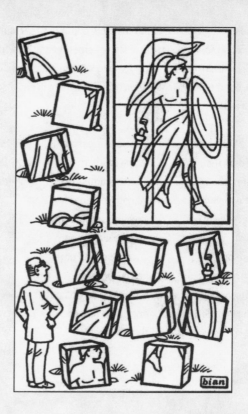

Answer on page 473

51 · CAUGHT NAPPING

Solve the clues given to find out the facts about five real murderers who might well have "gotten away with it" except for an odd twist of fate—sometimes their own folly. For instance, after committing a murder on a train, one man accidentally left behind his own hat and took the victim's! Another poisoned his wife, but then his friends as well, making them ill and leading to his arrest. Read on! The first clue has been entered for you.

1 Franz Muller died earlier than the murderer who was caught napping, not only because of his handwriting, but also because he left out the P in "Hampstead" in a note. Armstrong died the decade before Frederick.

2 Field confessed to two murders he didn't commit to get money from the newspapers. The first time he was freed, but the second time he was believed— and hung! He was not one of the first two of the five to die.

3 Manton, who died in 1947, was not Herbert, the poisoner.

HINT:
In which year did Field die? So who died in 1949?

4 Horace was not the one who died in 1949 after being convicted on the evidence of the only identifiable part of the remains of the victim's body—a gallstone!

Answer on page 473

FIRST NAME	SURNAME	YEAR DIED	CONVICTION
FRANZ	~~ARMSTRONG~~	1864	CONFESSION
	~~FIELD~~	1922	GALLSTONE
	~~HAIG~~	1936	HAT
	~~MANTON~~	1947	POISON
	(MULLER)	~~1949~~	~~SPELLING~~
FREDERICK	~~ARMSTRONG~~	~~1864~~	CONFESSION
	FIELD	~~1922~~	GALLSTONE
	HAIG	1936	HAT
	MANTON	1947	POISON
	~~MULLER~~	1949	SPELLING
HERBERT	ARMSTRONG	1864	CONFESSION
	FIELD	1922	GALLSTONE
	HAIG	1936	HAT
	MANTON	1947	POISON
	~~MULLER~~	1949	SPELLING
HORACE	ARMSTRONG	1864	CONFESSION
	FIELD	1922	GALLSTONE
	HAIG	1936	HAT
	MANTON	1947	POISON
	~~MULLER~~	1949	SPELLING
JOHN	ARMSTRONG	1864	CONFESSION
	FIELD	1922	GALLSTONE
	HAIG	1936	HAT
	MANTON	1947	POISON
	~~MULLER~~	1949	SPELLING

52 · BATTLESHIPS

Do you remember the old game of battleships? These puzzles are based on that idea. Your task is to find the vessels in the diagram. Some parts of boats or sea squares have already been filled in, and a number next to a row or column refers to the number of occupied squares in that row or column. The boats may be positioned horizontally or vertically, but no two boats or parts of boats are in adjacent squares—horizontally, vertically, or diagonally.

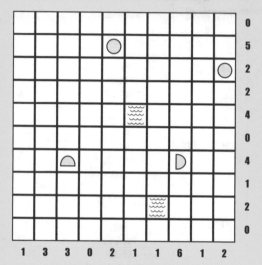

Aircraft carrier:

Battleships:

Cruisers:

Destroyers:

Answer on page 473

53 · SPOT THE BALL

Sarah has hidden a ball under one of the six teacups. Using the following information, can you say under which of the cups (1–6) Sarah has put the ball?

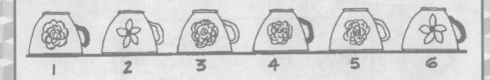

The cup hiding the ball has a cup with a white handle on its immediate left.

The cup hiding the ball has a cup with a rose pattern on its immediate right.

The cup hiding the ball has a different colored handle from the cup on its immediate left.

Answer on page 473

54 · FINE LINES

With one continuous line, join all the black camels (starting from number 1); with another continuous line, join all the white camels (starting from letter A). The lines must not cross!

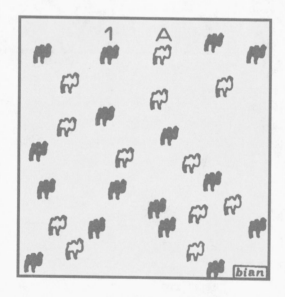

Answer on page 474

How many circles are needed to balance scale C?

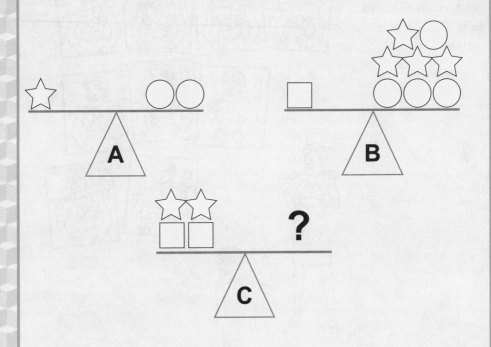

Answer on page 474

56 · SNAP IT UP

Which of the nine snapshots is the actual result of the picture taken by the photographer at the bottom?

bian

Answer on page 474

57 · LOGI-5

Each line, across and down, is to have each of the letters A, B, C, D, and E, appearing once each. Also, every shape—shown by the thick lines—must have each of the letters in it. Can you fill in the grid?

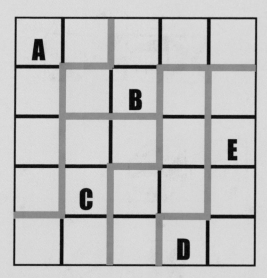

Which of the four numbered boxes is shown opened out at the top?

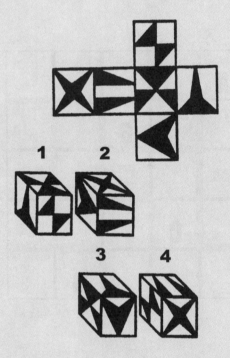

59 · MATCH THE HALVES

These soldiers are all mixed up! Can you match the halves?

Answer on page 474

60 · TWIN SET

These twins always like to have everything the same as each other, and are looking for two identical lamps. Can you spot them?

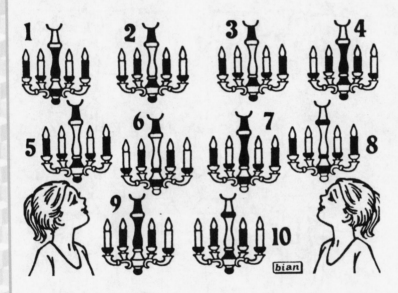

Answer on page 474

61 · FISHY TALE

Hugh took a photo of his son standing in front of the aquarium at the zoo.
Which fish in the tank is the same as the one in the photo?

Answer on page 474

62 · BIG TOP

Karl Krack, who owns a small traveling circus, believes that variety is the spice of life, and for each show he alters the order of his eight acts. Can you work out what the order will be for tonight's performance?

Fred the Fire-Eater is two acts after the Flying Fortresses and three acts before the Agilles Acrobats. Señor Pedro's Poodles are three acts before the Crazy Carvellos but after Madame Poll's Parrots, who are not starting the program. The Clever Clowns are three acts before Jim the Juggler but they are after Señor Pedro's Poodles.

1	2	3	4
5	6	7	8

Answer on page 474

63 · TWIT TWOO

Olly the owl and his five brothers, Oswald, Oscar, Owen, Orinoco, and Oleg are hanging around on a branch. Olly and Oscar are identical twins. Can you spot them?

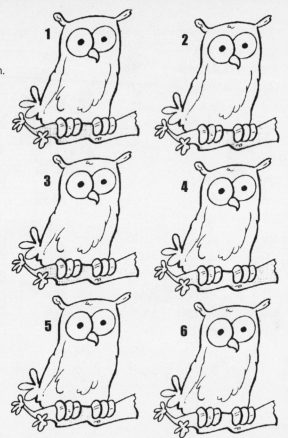

Answer on page 474

64 · NUMBER JIG

Fit the numbers into the grid as quickly as possible. We have given you some help.

3 figures	4 figures
120	2512
122	8300
125	8328
253	8476
254	
281	**5 figures**
283	10863
325	10875
326	11241
400	12248
527	12841
583	12845
800	14682
928	15572
	16163
	27891

30094
30627
40111
40491
41138
42710
43336
43868
43939
73093
78865
79941
83544
89233
90407
92248
96271

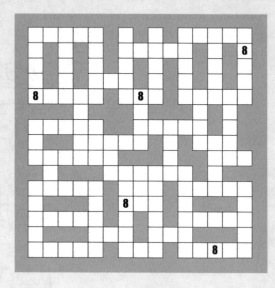

6 figures	251155	638471
250153	471206	738262

Answer on page 474

65 · BALANCING THE SCALES

How many stars are needed to balance scale C?

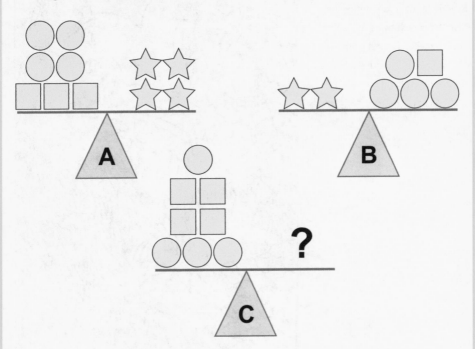

Answer on page 474

Humphrey Hunter has gone off looking for the disgusting Slop Monster, which turns its victims to slime when it catches them. Humph needs ten bullets to defend himself. Can you find them all in the picture?

Answer on page 474

Which point will be touched when the engineer turns the handle as shown?

Answer on page 475

68 · DROPOUT

The man is trying to buy a scarf. In the bottom picture he's made his choice. Which one did he buy?

Answer on page 475

69 · SUDOKU

Place a number from 1 to 9 in each empty square so that each row, each column, and each 3 x 3 block contain all the numbers from 1 to 9.

		1	8		6	7		
		7	3	4	9	6		
6	4			2			8	3
4	7						1	8
	9	8				5	7	
5	6						2	9
8	1			9			6	7
		6	2	1	7	8		
		9	6		4	1		

Answer on page 475

Have a careful look at this picture. How many complete circles can you see?

Answer on page 475

Match up the pairs of brothers using the information given.

Answer on page 475

Use your deductive reasoning to form a pathway from START to FINISH moving either horizontally or vertically (but not diagonally). The number at the beginning of every row or column indicates exactly how many boxes in that row or column your pathway must pass through. The small diagram is given as an example of how it works.

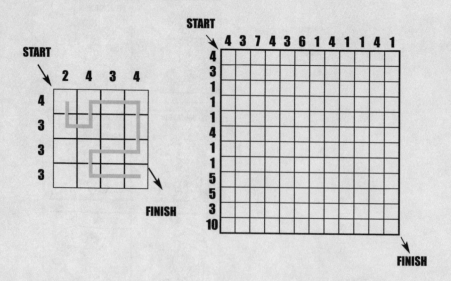

START

2 4 3 4

4
3
3
3

FINISH

START

4 3 7 4 3 6 1 4 1 1 4 1

4
3
1
1
1
4
1
1
5
5
3
10

FINISH

Answer on page 475

73 · MIRROR, MIRROR

Which three of the nine reversed images belong to Amy (A), Belinda (B), and Cathy (C), shown at the top?

Answer on page 475

This is an odd type of safe. If you solve all the clues and enter them in the grid, the correct combination will appear in the shaded squares.

ACROSS
1   Add 220 to 4 across
4   Multiply 21 down by 4
6   Multiply 23 across by 10
7   Subtract 200 from 1 across
9   Add 4 to 1 across
13 Add 666,581,666 to 6 across
17 Half of 13 across
20 Subtract 6,238 from 23 across
23 5 percent of 170,000
24 Add 36,262 to 12 down
25 Subtract 1 from 26 across
26 Next in series 715, 814, 913, ...

DOWN
1   Multiply 4 down by 10
2   Square 22
3   Add 100 to 4 down
4   First three digits of 26 across
5   Add 4,404 to 2 down
8   Subtract 4,999 from 10 down
10 Multiply 5 by 433,277
11 Add 26,033 to 23 down
12 Subtract 10,096 from 11 down
14 Add 60 to 15 down
15 Square root of 375,769
16 Second, third and fourth digits of
    11 down
18 Add 199 to 26 across
19 Add 991 to 25 across
21 Subtract 357 from 22 down
22 Square root of 369,664
23 Add 193 to 22 down

75 · LINE UP

With one continuous line, join all the white balls (starting from number 1, and with straight lines from ball to ball); and with another, join all the black balls (starting from A). The lines must not cross!

Answer on page 475

The man is trying to choose a briefcase. In the picture on the right, he has made his choice. Which briefcase did he choose?

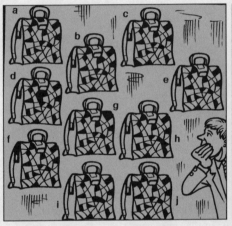 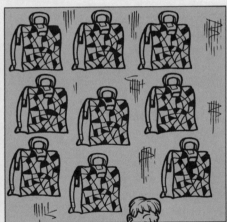

Answer on page 475

This is an odd type of safe. If you solve all the clues and enter them in the grid, the correct combination will appear in the shaded squares.

ACROSS

1. Add 5 across to 32 across
3. Subtract 765 from 1 across
5. First three digits of 26 down
7. Divide 31 across by 3
8. Multiply 7 across by 59
9. Add 4 to 4 down
11. Divide 17 down by 7 across
13. Multiply 18 down by 5
14. 3 percent of 646,700
16. Square 1 across
21. Square 34 across
22. 5 percent of 1,026,100
25. Square root of 40,401
27. Divide 6 down by 7 across
28. Subtract 31 across from 13 across
30. First three digits of 10 down
31. First two digits of 24 down
32. Add 692 to 33 across
33. Divide 32 across by 5
34. Subtract 103 from 1 across

DOWN

1. Add 7 across to 15 down
2. Subtract 7,457,863 from 10 down
4. Twice 5 across
5. Multiply 1 across by 2
6. Roman MM
9. Subtract 5,925,600 from 10 down
10. Add 8,159,550 to 15 down
12. First four digits of 2 down
15. Multiply half of 7 across by 1,981
17. Subtract 45 from 12 down
18. Square root of 12,321
19. Multiply 34 across by 3
20. Add 859,856 to 19 down
23. Months in ninety-and-a-half years
24. Divide 31 across by 2, then multiply by 25 across
26. Multiply the first two digits of 4 down by 51
29. Add 6 to 25 across

Answer on page 475

Karen moves to a new apartment, but almost regrets it when she discovers that the moving men have mislaid some of her possessions—six, to be exact—and have damaged one other. Which are missing, and which has been damaged?

Answer on page 475

79 · BATTLESHIPS

Do you remember the old game of battleships? These puzzles are based on that idea. Your task is to find the vessels in the diagram. Some parts of boats or sea squares have already been filled in, and a number next to a row or column refers to the number of occupied squares in that row or column. The boats may be positioned horizontally or vertically, but no two boats or parts of boats are in adjacent squares—horizontally, vertically, or diagonally.

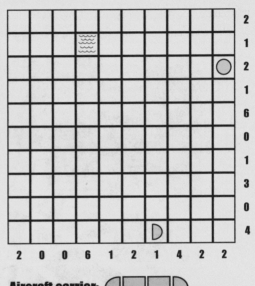

2
1
2
1
6
0
1
3
0
4

2 0 0 6 1 2 1 4 2 2

Aircraft carrier:

Battleships:

Cruisers:

Destroyers:

Answer on page 475

80 · PICKUP STICKS

In this puzzle, you have to imagine picking up each one of these six brooms in turn, but you can only pick the top one each time. In what order must you choose them?

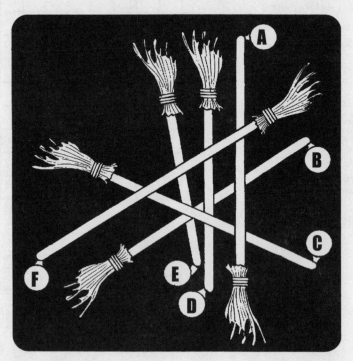

Answer on page 475

81 · SUDOKU

Place a number from 1 to 9 in each empty square so that each row, each column, and each 3x3 block contains all the numbers from 1 to 9.

				6			4	
	2		5				7	
1		3	9	8				
	9	4			3			7
2					9			3
	1	6			5			8
8		1	2	4				
	3		7				2	
				5			8	

Answer on page 476

82 · MIRROR, MIRROR

Which three reversed images belong to Alicia (A), Bernadette (B), and Claudia (C), who are shown at the top?

Answer on page 476

83 · NUMBER SQUARES

Can you place the numbers into the empty squares and make each equation (across and down) correct? Some are already in place.

The missing numbers are: 2, 3, 4, 5, 6, 7, 7, 8, 9, 13, and 35.

	+		=	
x		−		+
	x		=	
=		=		=
12	+		=	19

19	+		=	54
−		÷		÷
	−		=	3
=		=		=
11	+		=	18

Answer on page 476

This is an odd type of safe. If you solve all the clues and enter them in the grid, the correct combination will appear in the shaded squares.

ACROSS

2 Square 789

7 Multiply 258 by 87, add 6,316

8 Divide 996,366 by 14

9 Add 789 to 987, subtract 64

12 Cube 18, subtract 735

15 Septuagenarian minimum age

16 Ounces in 77 pounds

19 Subtract 1,234,567 from 33,197,828

23 Cube 213, multiply by 10

25 Multiply 97 by 79, subtract 515

27 Not quite a century

28 Divide 397,600 by 56, add 111

30 Add twenty percent of 3,185 to twenty-five percent of 2,584

32 Yards in sixteen-and-a-half miles

34 Add 37,216 to 51,030

36 Subtract 2 across from 1,221,393

DOWN

1 Square yards in an acre

2 Subtract one-ninth of 693 from 143

3 Twelve-and-a-half percent of 1,768

4 Multiply P's alphabetical position by Q's

5 Just shy of a dozen

6 Divide 264,627 by 27 across

10 Cube 198

11 Add 266,166 to 765,432

12 Triple 22 down

Answer on page 476

13 Add one-fifth of 226,645 to one-seventh of 335,755

14 Quadruple 17,792

16 Divide 22,194,844 by thirty-five per cent of 3,920

17 Multiply 237 by 85, add 1,157

18 Subtract the square of 14 from the cube of 6

20 Divide 20,152 by 22

21 Multiply 25 by 23, subtract 276

22 Square root of 289

24 Square root of 441

26 Add 873 to 1,125

29 Dunkirk date

30 Subtract one-third of 1,116 from a quarter of 1,924

31 Square 19, add 26

33 Subtract half-a-dozen from 12 down

35 Hours in 295,200 seconds

Find eight differences between these pictures.

Answer on page 476

86 · COG-ITATE

Which of the four weights will rise and which will fall when the handle is turned as shown?

Answer on page 476

87 · TREASURE HUNT

The small piece of the map at the top shows under which large bush the treasure is buried. Can you work out in which square this is on the larger map?

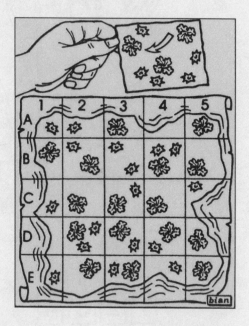

Answer on page 476

Which one of these six photographs of Mandy was taken as she posed in the bottom left-hand corner?

bian

Answer on page 476

89 · NUMBER JIG

Fit the numbers into the grid as quickly as possible.
One has been done for you.

3 figures	5662	51329
182	7353	60138
189	8326	63258
192		70910
219	**5 figures**	80809
238	13802	81101
304	17608	86065
381	17974	87552
410	19344	90804
560	23509	91505
565	23916	92108
~~597~~	24415	92316
763	26231	98184
835	28398	99215
897	39264	
	47028	**6 figures**
4 figures	47119	327453
3294	50264	518007

6 figures 613254
810871
951326

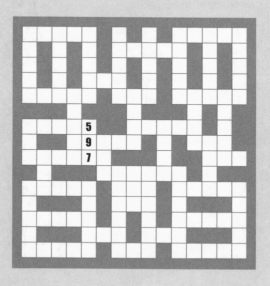

Answer on page 476

100

Roberto's violin bow is at the bottom of the pile. Can you work out which one it is?

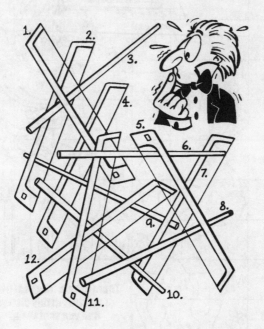

Answer on page 476

Answer on page 476

92 · LOGI-PATH

Use your deductive reasoning to form a pathway from START to FINISH moving either horizontally or vertically (but not diagonally). The number at the beginning of every row or column indicates exactly how many boxes in that row or column your pathway must pass through. The small diagram is given as an example of how it works.

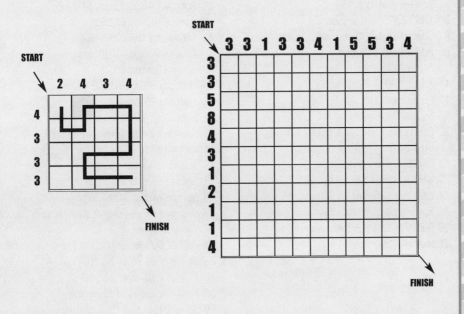

START

2 4 3 4

4
3
3
3

FINISH

START

3 3 1 3 3 4 1 5 5 3 4

3
3
5
8
4
3
1
2
1
1
4

FINISH

Answer on page 477

93 · SAFE BET

This is an odd type of safe. If you solve all the clues and enter them in the grid, the correct combination will appear in the shaded squares.

ACROSS

1   Square root of 4 down
5   Square root of 1,936
7   Add 12,178 to 8 across
8   Ounces in 1,253 pounds
9   Add 900 to 1 across
10 Twice 23 across
13 Add 1,000 to 22 down
16 Square 2 down
20 Square 24 down
21 Divide 29 down by 3, then multiply by 1,051
23 Add 1,881 to 26 down
25 Next in series 95, 104, 113, ...
27 Last five digits of 20 across
28 Subtract 4,080 from 15 down
30 Subtract 20 from 5 across
31 Multiply 1 across by 5

DOWN

1   Square root of 3 down
2   Subtract 40,193 from 11 down
3   Square root of 28,561
4   Subtract 1 from 25 across
5   First four digits of 10 down
6   Twice 30 across
10 Multiply 29 down by 2,967
11 Multiply 29 down by 2,763
12 Subtract 16,250 from 11 down
13 Subtract 24,229 from 14 down
14 Add 4,126 to 27 across
15 Subtract 4 from 10 down
17 Square last two digits of 27 across
18 Square root of 504,100
19 Subtract three times 1 down from 17 down
22 Twice 2 down
24 Half of 5 down
25 Multiply 29 down by 10
26 Multiply 30 across by 10
27 First two digits of 21 across
29 Square root of 225

Answer on page 477

94 · POT LUCK

Which of the numbered pots should logically occupy the empty square?

Answer on page 477

The Groggins Gang celebrates another successful caper—but can you be successful in discovering which two of the five details shown below (which might be displayed at a different angle from the original) belong to which two villains?

Answer on page 477

Can you discover the logical sequence shown here and work out what number should replace the question mark?

Answer on page 477

97 · HALF AND HALF

Here are nine mixed-up pots. Can you match up the black left halves with their white counterparts?

Answer on page 477

98 · CIRCLE OF DIGITS

The figure below consists of three concentric circles divided into eight sectors; the three single-digit numbers in each sector add up to 15. The circles will be referred to as outer, middle, and inner and one number in the inner has been inserted to give you a start. From the clues given, can you insert all the other numbers?

1 The only 0 appears in the outer circle, where there is no 1 or 3; there is no 9 in the middle and no number is repeated in any sector or circle.

2 All the numbers in sectors A and B are odd; B outer is one more than C inner and one less than H middle, which is one more than H inner; B inner is one less than G outer.

3 The 6 in the outer circle is diagonally opposite the 6 in the inner.

4 C inner is double D inner, while D outer is double D middle; F outer is double F middle, which is double G middle and the same as C outer; E outer is the same as A middle.

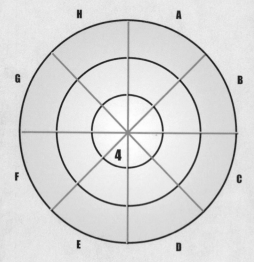

Starting tip: Work out the number in C inner.

Answer on page 477

99 · IN OILS

Which two of these numbered drawings show the same palette and the same picture, which two the same palette but a different picture, and which two a different palette but the same picture?

Answer on page 477

100 · HOW FEW?

What is the smallest group of people you can have that contains all these relationships?

aunt   brother   cousin   daughter   father
mother   nephew   niece   sister   son   uncle

Answer on page 478

101 · ROYALIST REVELS

The cavaliers have fought their battles and are relaxing after a huge victory. Two of them have a special reason for celebration—they were the only comrades to share the same battles, as their identical medals bear witness. Who are they?

Answer on page 478

102 · POUR TRICK

A very old puzzle is still sometimes dragged out at parties or in bars—especially as a way to win an easy bet. A full wine bottle is placed on the table. It has its cork in place and its plastic seal is unbroken. The perpetrator of the plot then claims to be able to drink wine from the bottle—without removing the seal or the cork and without smashing the bottle. You now have two choices—win the bet by telling the trickster how it can be done or lose the bet and look up the answer.

Answer on page 478

103 · DROPOUT

The man is choosing a T-shirt. In the right-hand picture, he's made his choice. Which T-shirt did he buy?

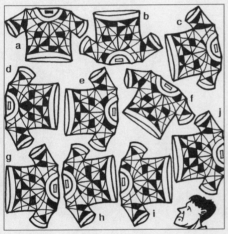 

Answer on page 478

104 · GOAL GETTER

Follow the correct path to help Sport
score a goal!

Answer on page 478

Can you match each cowboy to his son?

Answer on page 478

106 · BALL GAME

Can you place these cannonballs in order; from the ball nearest to the cannon to the ball furthest from the cannon?

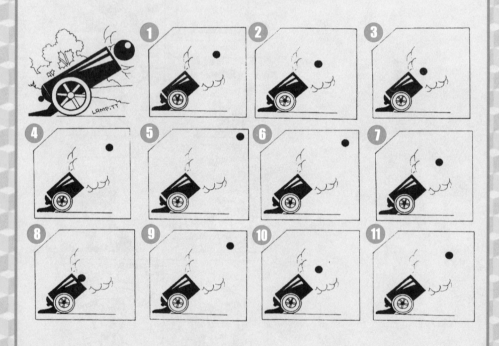

Answer on page 478

107 · DIVIDE THE SHAPES

Can you divide the picture below by drawing
three straight lines to produce four sections,
each containing nine different shapes?

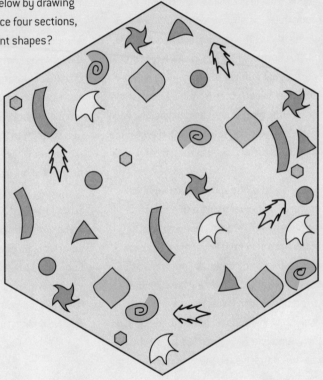

Answer on page 478

108 · A BRIDGE TOO FAR

Eight men and eight women are playing bridge at four tables, as shown. In the game at hand, dummy is in a different position at each table, and the contract at each is in a different suit and for a different number of tricks—this number also differs in each case from the table number. With the following clues, can you position each person, and also say who is dummy and name the contract being played at each table?

Roger (South) is dummy at his table, which is numbered one lower than Connie's and one higher than Harry's, both of whom are in a different position from Roger and from each other, neither being dummy. Fred and Gordon are partners at the remaining table, neither being dummy. Alan (West) is at a table where the contract is 4 spades. Tessa (dummy) is one table counterclockwise from Eddie, at whose table the contract is for one trick more than on table 1.

Answer on page 478

Dummy at table 4 is the person whose name comes first alphabetically at that table. Jane and Dot are in the same position at different tables whose numbers are two apart; this is also true of Kate and Lola, the first-named in each case being at the lower-numbered table. From his seat Peter, who is not at table 2, can see table 2, but not table 4; his contract is in diamonds, while Michael's table is going for hearts, but one fewer.

Susie (dummy) has Jane on her left and Harry on her right; her partner is Peter, and the contract is for one more than the table number. Connie has Dot on her left, who is not in the same position as Fred. Tessa, whose table is playing a red-suit contract, is in the same relative position as Babs.

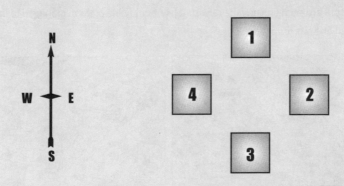

	Table 1	Table 2	Table 3	Table 4
N				
E				
S				
W				
Contract				

109 · DROPOUT

Ten competitors are seen starting the race (left), but only nine of them managed to finish it (right). Which one has dropped out?

Answer on page 478

110 · BATTLESHIPS

Do you remember the old game of battleships? These puzzles are based on that idea. Your task is to find the vessels in the diagram. Some parts of boats or sea squares have already been filled in, and a number next to a row or column refers to the number of occupied squares in that row or column. The boats may be positioned horizontally or vertically, but no two boats or parts of boats are in adjacent squares—horizontally, vertically, or diagonally.

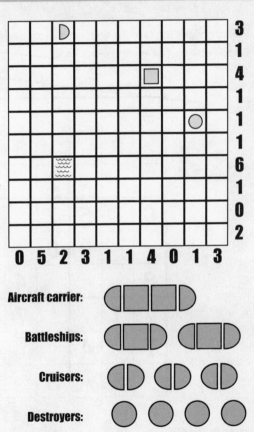

Aircraft carrier:

Battleships:

Cruisers:

Destroyers:

111 · SUDOKU

Place a number from 1 to 9 in each empty square so that each row, each column, and each 3x3 block contains all the numbers from 1 to 9.

9								
	8			6		1	2	
			2				8	
6		5	7		3			
		9	6				7	
8				4	5	2		
	1			7	4			
7		4					1	
	5		3		8			4

Answer on page 479

124

Fit the numbers into the grid as quickly as possible. One has been done for you.

3 figures	5215	231456
119	5907	254329
~~238~~	6899	371924
308	7606	406138
483	9814	432901
576		470719
698	**5 figures**	523250
801	13508	618383
993	24134	634205
	29501	713248
4 figures	31886	893071
1031	54396	900102
2801	65908	942603
3558	89099	964131
3560		
3992	**6 figures**	
4376	106112	
4882	125388	

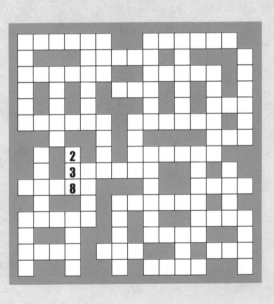

Answer on page 479

The numbers in each hexagon add up to the same total. Can you work out what that is, by finding the correct value for each symbol?

Answer on page 479

Mary and Martin are in space today, and they've crash-landed. Luckily, a friendly alien is at hand! Put the blocks on the left into the correct order to find out what it is.

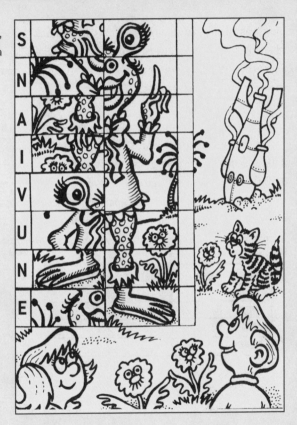

Answer on page 479

115 · PASS

There was an unusual result this year at Claggthorpe's Hobbyist Competition—all four competitors ended up with just 13 points each. After a quick chat among the judges, it was announced that the contestant with the fewest number of passes would be the winner. Can you work out who that was?

1 The post-person who had specialized in Stone Age Poetry had one fewer passes than Wendy Dee who is not the police officer.

2 Hugh Seddit had one more pass than the specialist in Soap Operas.

3 Watt Wazzit had specialized in the life and times of Bernard Gribble (his great-uncle) but he is not the barperson who had four passes.

4 The man who specialized in Bolton Brickworks of the late 18th century is not the shopkeeper who had one fewer passes than Ivor Started.

NAME	JOB	SUBJECT	PASSES
HUGH			
IVOR			
WATT			
WENDY			

Answer on page 479

116 · MIX 'N' MATCH

These fellows are having a bad day!
Match the correct halves to remake
them.

Answer on page 479

Can you match each husband to his wife?

Answer on page 479

Can you draw three straight lines, each one drawn from one edge to another, so that they divide the box into five sections each containing a cup and a saucer?

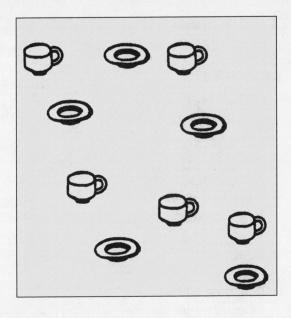

Answer on page 479

This is an odd type of safe. If you solve all the clues and enter them in the grid, the correct combination will appear in the shaded squares.

ACROSS

2 First four digits of 16 across

6 Subtract 28 down from 6 down

8 Subtract 1 from 1 down

9 Add 61 to 34 across

12 Add 3 to 2 across

14 Multiply 6 across by 33 down

16 Multiply 12 across by 33 down, then subtract 23

18 Square 6 down

22 3,992,004 multiplied by 5 down

24 15 percent of 613,700

25 Subtract 41,546 from 24 across

26 First four digits of 22 across

29 Add 23 down to 32 across, then subtract 1,000

31 Subtract 33 down from 1 down

32 Add 117 to 2 across

34 Twice 28 down

DOWN

1 Square root of 34 across

3 Square root of 110,889

4 Multiply 3 down by 3

5 Divide 34 across by the square of 33 down

6 Square 1 down, then add 7,285

7 Multiply 1 down by 20,467,900

10 Subtract 189,171,485 from 7 down

11 Divide 6 down by 5

12 Multiply 16 by 68,241

13 Square 9 across, then add 5,367,136

15 Add 25,975 to 17 down

Answer on page 479

17 1,623 multiplied by a score
19 Multiply 1 down by 33 down, then add 7
20 Subtract 21 from 3 down
21 Divide 23 down by 4
23 Multiply 4 down by 8
27 Add 3 to 3 down
28 Multiply 1 down by 20
30 Add 12 to 1 down
33 Divide 1 down by 4

The three fishes shown at the top can be seen in silhouette. Which silhouette belongs to which fish?

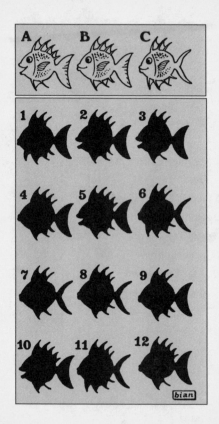

Answer on page 480

121 · SAMPLER

A sample has been cut from each of the three rolls of cloth. Which sample belongs to which roll?

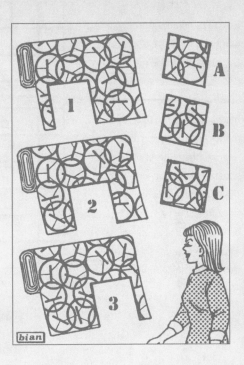

Answer on page 480

122 · BATTLESHIPS

Do you remember the old game of battleships? These puzzles are based on that idea. Your task is to find the vessels in the diagram. Some parts of boats or sea squares have already been filled in, and a number next to a row or column refers to the number of occupied squares in that row or column. The boats may be positioned horizontally or vertically, but no two boats or parts of boats are in adjacent squares—horizontally, vertically, or diagonally.

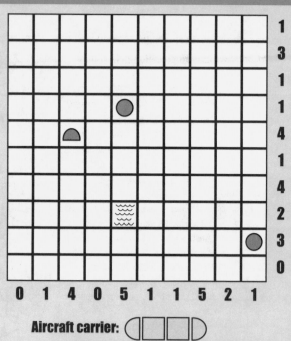

1
3
1
1
4
1
4
2
3
0

0 1 4 0 5 1 1 5 2 1

Aircraft carrier:

Battleships:

Cruisers:

Destroyers:

Answer on page 480

123 · LOGI-PATH

Use your deductive reasoning to form a pathway from START to FINISH moving either horizontally or vertically (but not diagonally). The number at the beginning of every row or column indicates exactly how many boxes in that row or column your pathway must pass through. The small diagram is given as an example of how it works.

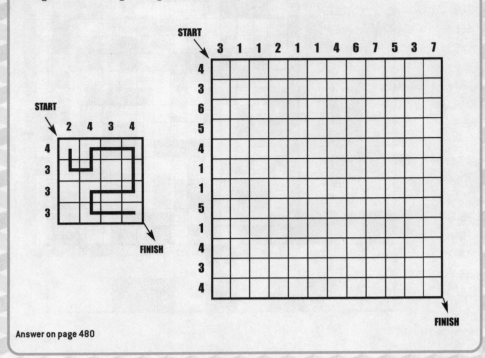

Answer on page 480

124 · NUMBER JIG

Fit the numbers into the grid as quickly as possible. One has been done for you.

3 figures	6799	356174
193	6839	389077
285	7443	421864
556	8304	478321
586	9389	508116
638		512630
234	**5 figures**	553681
817	28946	603845
929	29280	612349
	40665	745723
4 figures	56833	765381
1064	57813	850337
1880	72353	900964
2586	89936	953341
3060		
4992	**6 figures**	
5365	145637	
5813	288016	

Answer on page 480

125 · DARTING ABOUT

A dart player scores 83 with three darts hitting a triple, a double, and a single. Given that the three numbers that he hits add up to 38 and that the difference between the largest and smallest numbers is 9, can you work out how his score is made up?

Triple   Double   Single

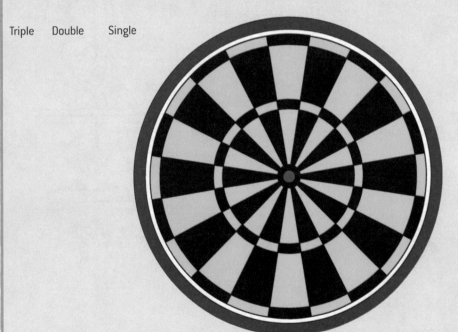

Answer on page 480

Can you match each man to his brother?

Answer on page 480

127 · SIX-WAY COUNT

How many regular hexagons of all sizes are there in this diagram?

Answer on page 480

128 · BLACKOUT

Which three insects are shown in silhouette at the top?

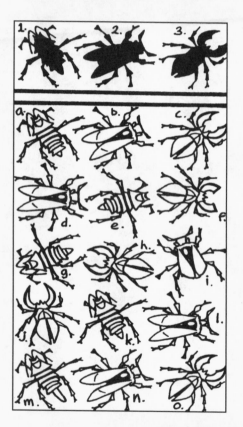

Answer on page 480

Connect the dots from 1 to 37 to reveal the hidden picture.

130 · COG-ITATE

Can you see which two weights will rise and which two will fall when the man turns the lever as shown?

Answer on page 480

131 · BATTLESHIPS

Do you remember the old game of battleships? This puzzle is based on that idea. Your task is to find the vessels in the diagram. Some parts of boats or sea squares have already been filled in, and a number next to a row or column refers to the number of occupied squares in that row or column. The boats may be positioned horizontally or vertically, but no two boats or parts of boats are in adjacent squares—horizontally, vertically, or diagonally.

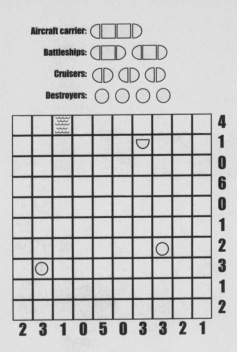

Aircraft carrier:

Battleships:

Cruisers:

Destroyers:

4
1
0
6
0
1
2
3
1
2

2 3 1 0 5 0 3 3 2 1

Answer on page 480

132 · SAFE BET

This is an odd type of safe. If you solve all the clues and enter them in the grid, the correct combination will appear in the shaded squares.

ACROSS

1 Multiply 32 by 23
3 Subtract 3,939 from 4,815
5 Multiply 21 by 12
7 Multiply H's alphabetical position by L's
8 Cube 7, add 7
9 Two-nineteenths of 7,467
11 Add a gross, a score, and a baker's dozen
13 Minutes between 7:35 p.m. and 2:25 a.m.
14 Add 12,345 to 13,033
16 Three-sevenths of 784,917
21 Square 999
22 Add 14 across to 68,804
25 Divide 4,215 by the square root of 225
27 Triple 30 percent of 950
28 Subtract 697 from two-thirds of 1,857

DOWN

1 Divide 199,850 by 25
2 Add 99,999 to 595,033
4 Pounds in 7 hundredweights and 1 stone
5 A quarter of 5,104 plus a half of 2,474
6 Cube 9, add 4,348
9 Add 3,993,993 to 3,968,932
10 Subtract 1,591,591 from 7,890,672
12 Multiply 487 by 16, add 100
15 Divide 58,630 by 11

30 Add the square root of 729 to 729
31 Number of face cards in 6 packs
32 Divide 9,462 by 19, subtract 99
33 17 percent of 500, plus 216
34 Square 17, add 605

Answer on page 481

17 Two-thirds of 5,697
18 Add one-seventh of 1,099 to one-eighth of 1,288
19 Divide 16,785 by 9, add 33
20 Quadruple 78,182
23 Multiply 4 down by 8, subtract 1,805
24 Subtract two-ninths of 8,379 from 3,421
26 Date of start of World War I
29 A score of scores, plus a score

133 · BATTLESHIPS

Do you remember the old game of battleships? This puzzle is based on that idea. Your task is to find the vessels in the diagram. Some parts of boats or sea squares have already been filled in, and a number next to a row or column refers to the number of occupied squares in that row or column. The boats may be positioned horizontally or vertically, but no two boats or parts of boats are in adjacent squares—horizontally, vertically, or diagonally.

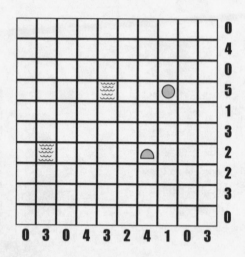

Aircraft carrier:

Battleships:

Cruisers:

Destroyers:

Answer on page 481

134 · POT SHOT

Two of these pictures are identical, while each of the others is different in one small detail. Which are the "twins" and what are the differences?

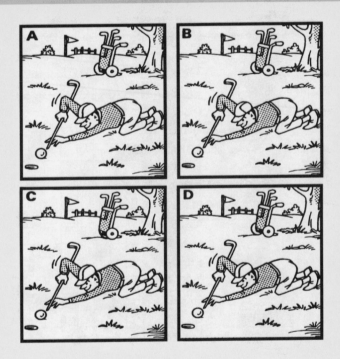

Answer on page 481

135 · NUMBER JIG

Fit the numbers into the grid as quickly as possible. One has been done for you.

3 figures

157
298
380
541
696
909
913
974

6309
6312
6923
7008
7623
8059
8335
8790
9174

49933
65248
66302
68411
75120
82714
83307
91369
95505

4 figures

1670
1810
2031
2085
3291
4108
4328
5364

5 figures

13556
18244
25054
27305
30393
31011
33906
44815

6 figures

210954
360610
540132
652224
708357
880346

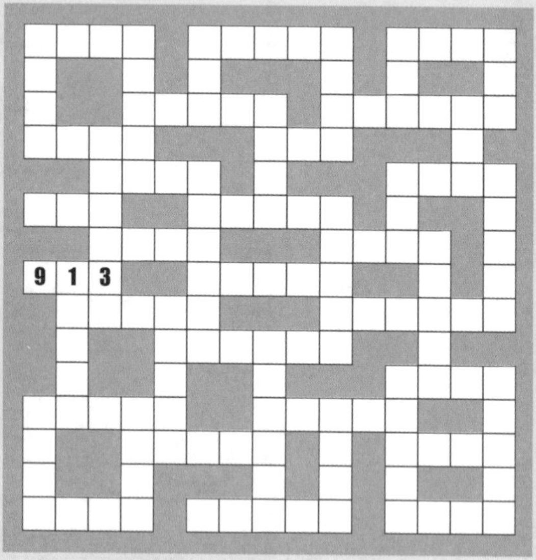

Answer on page 481

136 · WIRED UP

Can you work out which of the four plugs is connected to the shaver?

Answer on page 481

137 · TRILINES

Which three straight lines, drawn from border to border, divide the box into five parts, each containing two kangaroos?

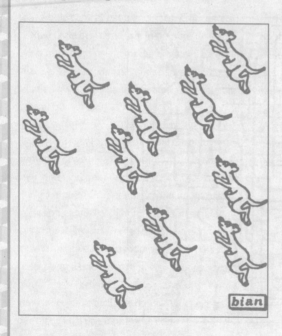

Answer on page 481

Which of these photos is actually of the model shown?

Answer on page 481

139 · COG-ITATE

Which one of the two points will be touched
when the engineer turns the handle as shown?

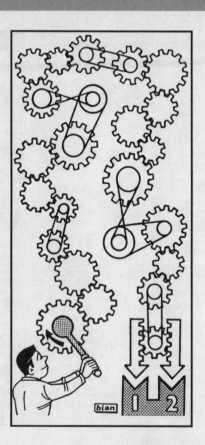

Answer on page 481

140 · BALL BOY

Danny's mother took a photo of him with his favorite ball. Which ball in the larger picture is the same as the one in the photo?

Answer on page 481

141 · IDENTICAL PAIRS

Fido was really in the doghouse when he grabbed a snack earlier this week! Can you find six pairs of identical squares here?

Answer on page 481

Using the totals, calculate the price of each cup, tube of toothpaste, towel, and bar of soap.

$6.20

$7.50

$2.70

$7.40

143 · IDENTICAL TWINS

Which two musicians below are identical?

Answer on page 481

Which one of the four numbered pieces should logically replace the question mark in this design?

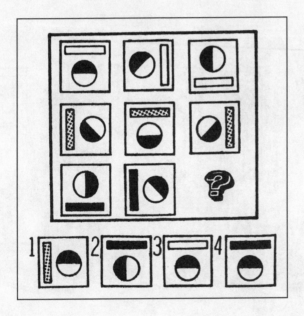

Answer on page 481

Our illustrator has made ten errors in this scene—some of them obvious, others not so easy to spot. Can you identify them all?

Answer on page 482

146 · BOXED IN

Can you see which three objects appear
in all four boxes?

Answer on page 482

Each of these eight pictures is missing a detail that is present in the other seven. Can you spot all eight missing details?

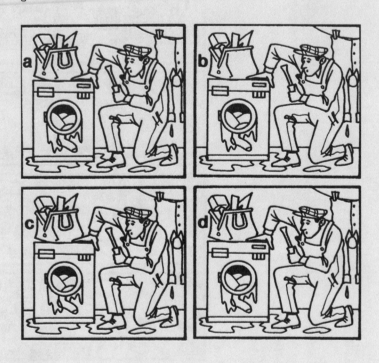

Answer on page 482

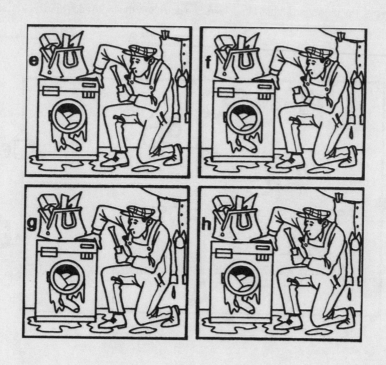

148 · MAN HUNT

Each hunter A, B, C, D, E has trekked across the frozen waste and is now in his hut—a, b, c, d, e. Naturally, the hut letter corresponds to the hunter's. At no time at all did anyone's tracks cross anyone else's. Nor did anyone cross either lake. Can you show the route each man took?

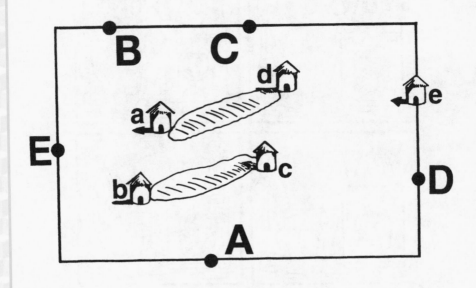

Answer on page 482

149 · CARRYOUT

Each picture is lacking in one detail that is present in the other three. What are they?

Answer on page 482

150 · LOGI-PATH

Use your deductive reasoning to form a pathway from START to FINISH moving either horizontally or vertically (but not diagonally). The number at the beginning of every row or column indicates exactly how many boxes in that row or column your pathway must pass through. The small diagram is given as an example of how it works.

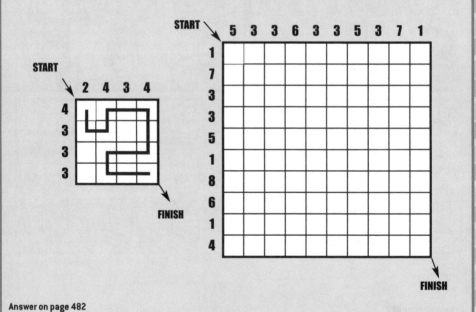

Answer on page 482

151 · FLAG DAY

Arthur's flag is the same shape as Ben's, and his flagpole is the same as Colin's but not the same as Damien's. Arthur is wearing a gray neckerchief, and Errol has one with stripes. Match the names to the numbers!

Answer on page 482

Can you find the detail missing from each picture that is present in the other three?

Answer on page 482

Place a number from 1 to 9 in each empty square so that each row, each column, and each 3x3 block contains all the numbers from 1 to 9.

				7				
	1	4	6		3	8	5	
	9		2	4	7		6	
1		6				5		4
3	8			5			4	9
	2	9	4		8	3	7	
6			3		1			5

Answer on page 482

Two of these go-carts and riders are identical. Which two?

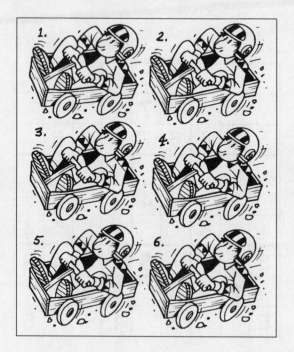

Answer on page 482

155 · IN THE MAIL

Four housewife neighbors in a suburban area of an American town each had a different colored mailbox at the entrance to her property. From the clues given below, can you work out the name of the woman who lives at each address, and work out the color of her mailbox?

Clues

1 The green mailbox is next to Gemma's on one side, and Mrs. Gerber's on the other.

2 Arlene chose the yellow mailbox for her gate, at a house with a higher number than Mrs. Fishbein's.

3 The red mailbox is at Mrs. Baron's house.

4 The blue mailbox is on the gate of number 232, which is not Louise's home.

First names: Arlene; Gemma; Kate; Louise
Surnames: Baron; Fishbein; Flint; Gerber
Mailboxes: blue; green; red; yellow

Starting tip: Begin by placing the green mailbox.

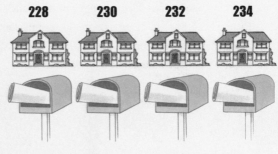

228   **230**   **232**   **234**

First name: _____ _____ _____ _____

Surname: _____ _____ _____ _____

Color: _____ _____ _____ _____

Answer on page 482

156 · STAG NIGHT

It was the eve of Tom Toper's wedding, and his pals were determined to have some fun. They celebrated in each of the five bars in their town. Can you discover the order in which they visited each bar, the name of the bartender, and the location of each bar?

Clues

A The evening started at the Golden Goose and finished in Gasworks Lane.

B The Green Dragon was not the next port of call after the Black Bull in Mill Street.

C Toby Jugge served the party earlier than Ivor Goodale in Factory Road, but later than Jean-Ann Tonic at the Red Lion.

D Ava Nother could consider herself fortunate that the party visited her establishment before the bar in Waterworks Alley.

Answer on page 483

	Black Bull	Golden Goose	Green Dragon	Red Lion	White Horse	Ava Nother	Ivor Goodale	Jean-Ann Tonic	Phil Emupp	Toby Jugge	Factory Road	Gasworks Lane	Mill Street	Railway Approach	Waterworks Alley
First															
Second															
Third															
Fourth															
Fifth															
Factory Road															
Gasworks Lane															
Mill Street															
Railway Approach															
Waterworks Alley															
Ava Nother															
Ivor Goodale															
Jean-Ann Tonic															
Phil Emupp															
Toby Jugge															

Record in this grid all the information obtained from the clues, by using a cross to indicate a definite "no" and a tick to show a definite "yes." Transfer these to all sections of the grid thus eliminating all but one possibility, which must be the correct one.

Order	Name of bar	Bartender	Location

157 · ARTY ANNIE

Look at this simply divine mural that Annie's done. Can you find the continuous black line from the pom-pom on the skier's hat to Annie's brush?

Answer on page 483

The numbers alongside each row or column tell you how many blocks of black squares are in a line. For example: 2, 3, 5 tells you that from left to right (or top to bottom) there is a group of two black squares, then at least one white space, then a group of three black squares, then at least one white square, then a group of five black squares. Each block of black squares on the same line must have at least one white square between it and the next block of black squares.

Sometimes it is possible to tell which squares are going to be black without reference to other lines or columns. In the example below, we can deduce that any block of six black squares must incorporate the two central squares:

6

Can you complete this hanjie puzzle to reveal the hidden pattern or picture?

	2	6	3 1	2 1 3 1	2 3 2	2 1 3 2	1 4 1 1	1 1 2 1 2	1 2 6 1	1 2 1	1 6	2 4	2 4	7	4
2															
2															
3 2 3															
5 2 4															
2 2 3 1															
1 1 3 2															
1 2 4															
3 7															
2 3 6															
1 2 3															
7															
2 2															
1 1															
1 1															
3 3															

Answer on page 483

159 · TRIO

Three of the vases on the right are identical. Can you spot which three?

Three friends who were artists each produced a work showing a different feature of the village they all lived in. From the clues given below, can you identify the three, say which view each chose to depict, and work out the medium in which each worked?

Clues

1 Ms. Frame chose the village church as her subject.

2 Rosalind, whose surname is not Canvass, produced the oil painting.

3 The windmill was the subject of the watercolor painting, which was not the work of Nadine.

4 The pond was not the view selected by the artist who favored pen and ink for her picture.

	Canvass	Frame	Pallett	Pond	Village church	Windmill	Oils	Pen and ink	Watercolor
Josephine									
Nadine									
Rosalind									
Oils									
Pen and ink									
Watercolor									
Pond									
Village church									
Windmill									

First name	Surname	View	Medium

Answer on page 483

161 · SPOT THE DIFFERENCES

Ever since the British Parliament was founded its politicians have enjoyed a good shout at each other! See if you can spot eight differences between the two pictures.

Answer on page 483

There are eight differences between
the two cartoons. Can you spot them?

Answer on page 483

The names of eight planets have been broken in two. Can you put them back together again?

	EA	JUPI	
TO	VEN	MER	SAT
NUS	URN	US	TER
CURY	RS	PLU	RTH
	URA	MA	

Answer on page 484

Watch out King Harold, or you'll be history! Hidden in the background are 10 arrows. See if you can spot them all.

Answer on page 484

165 · DON'T PAY THE PIPER...

The diagram shows the Pied Piper leading away the children of Hamelin after the town refused to pay him for ridding it of rats. From the clues given below, can you name the first four children in the line, work out their ages, and say what work their father does in the town?

1 The cowherd's child is directly behind six-year-old Gretchen as they follow the Piper.

2 Hans is younger than Johann.

3 The boy who leads the line is not immediately followed by the butcher's child.

4 The child aged seven is third in the line.

5 Maria, whose father is an apothecary, is younger than the child in the second position.

Names: Gretchen; Hans; Johann; Maria

Ages: 5; 6; 7; 8

Father: apothecary; butcher; cowherd; woodcutter

Starting tip: Start by placing Gretchen.

Name: _____ _____ _____ _____

Age: _____ _____ _____ _____

Father: _____ _____ _____ _____

Answer on page 484

166 · RAM-PARTS

The scene on the right is reproduced below in twelve pieces, three of which have one detail more and four one detail less than the corresponding part of the original. Which details are extra and which are missing?

Answer on page 484

167 · SOMETHING FISHY

Four boys were fishing for carp in a shallow stream, each wearing a different-colored pair of boots. From the clues given below, can you identify the boys in positions 1 to 4, and work out the color of the boots each was wearing?

1 The boy in the red boots is somewhere to the left of Shaun, whose surname is not Brook.
2 Darren Poole is somewhere to the right of the youth in the brown boots.
3 Wader number 3 is Johnny, but the surname of the lad in position 2 is not Burne.
4 The green boots are worn by the boy wading alongside Garry; Waters is standing next to his friend, whose boots are black.

First names: Darren; Garry; Johnny; Shaun
Surnames: Brook; Burne; Poole; Waters
Boots: black; brown; green; red

Starting tip: Start by working out the first name of the boy in position 1.

Answer on page 484

First name: _____ _____ _____ _____

Surname: _____ _____ _____ _____

Boots: _____ _____ _____ _____

This is an odd type of safe. If you solve all the clues and enter them in the grid, the correct combination will appear in the shaded squares.

ACROSS
1   Subtract 2 from 24 squared
3   Add 7 to 8 across
5   Square 23, add 6
7   Divide 657 by 9
8   Divide 10,465 by 13
9   Multiply 27 across by 4, add 9
11   Multiply 78 by 3 squared
13   Triple 333
14   Fifteen per cent of 21 across, subtract 14
16   Square 546, add 8
21   Minutes in a leap year
22   Multiply 3,007 by 18
25   Two-thirds of 1,473, subtract 29
27   Add 66 to the square root of 1 down
28   Blackbirds in the pie multiplied by 10
30   VII times XIX
31   Ali Baba plus his thieves
32   Ten times a baker's dozen
33   Two-thirds of 732
34   Square 11, multiply by 3, subtract from 1,143

DOWN
1   Square 29 down, divide by 36
2   Multiply 19,197 by 25
4   Multiply square root of 289 by 8
5   Three-fifths of 8,450
6   26 down plus 12 dozen
9   2,349,116 plus 3,133,146
10   Multiply 31,817 by 9 score
12   Divide 70,912 by 32, subtract 7
15   7,513 plus 19 down
17   Add 5,792 to 26 down
18   25 percent of 468
19   Seoul falls to Communists
20   Subtract 323,492 from 932,709
23   Add 65 squared to 88
24   Pluto discovered
26   Multiply 96 by 35
29   One-eighth of 6 down

Answer on page 484

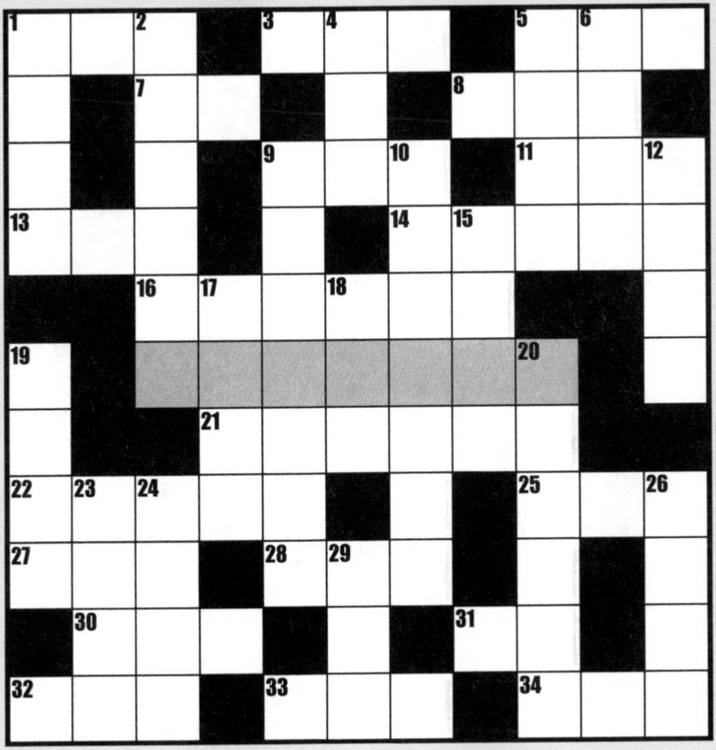

169 · FLIGHT FRIGHT

Each picture is lacking in one detail that is present in the other seven. Can you spot these details?

Answer on page 484

Who can this shady-looking character be? Match his left side to his right side to find out his name.

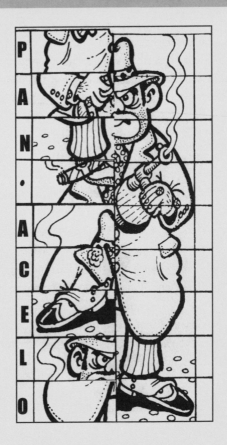

Answer on page 485

171 · PANDORA'S BOXES

Pandora Persimmons is the host of a quiz show in which successful contestants earn the right to open one of the boxes displayed as in the diagram, the contents of which may prove to be worth having or virtually worthless. Pandora tempts the contestants to forfeit the right to open by offering sums of money which, in this instance, were refused. From the clues given below, can you indicate in the diagram in what order each of our six qualified to open a box, which box each chose, and what it contained?

Clues

1　The order of the contestants did not tally with the number of the box each chose to open.

2　Lynne, who opened box 2, won a cash prize but less than that won by Sharon, whose turn was more than one earlier.

3　Michael, whose turn was next after that of the winner of $100, opened a box more than one place farther right than the big winner's.

4　The box containing the bar of soap turned out to be just left of the one opened by the fifth contestant; the box chosen by Jim was farther left than either.

Answer on page 485

5 The turn of the contestant who collected the wooden spoon was just before that of the one who was less than ecstatic at winning 50 cents; the box with the spoon in it was next right to the one holding $1,000.

6 Susan opened the box just right of that chosen by Rob, whose turn immediately followed hers.

7 No two men opened adjacent boxes; the winner of the big prize of $5,000 was the only person whose box was between a man's, on the left, and a woman's, on the right.

Contestants: Jim; Lynne; Michael; Rob; Sharon; Susan
Contents: 50 cents; $100; $1,000; $5,000; bar of soap; wooden spoon

Starting tip: Work out in which box the $5,000 was hidden.

Name:	——	——	——	——	——	——
Order:	——	——	——	——	——	——
Prize:	——	——	——	——	——	——

172 · SAFE BET

This is an odd type of safe. If you solve all the clues and enter them in the grid, the correct combination will appear in the shaded squares.

ACROSS

1   Boiling point in Fahrenheit
3   Multiply 16 by 14
5   Subtract 12 down from 15 cubed
7   Roman XXIX
8   Divide 24 down by 7 across
9   Add one score to 28 across
11 Double the square of 11
13 26 percent of 1,650
14 Feet in 3,673 yards
16 Multiply 33 across by 26 down
21 Subtract 19 down from 16 across
22 Cube Hitchcock's *Steps*
25 Multiply 31 across by 57
27 Quadruple the reverse digits of 25 across
28 Square root of 376,996

30 Subtract 9,000 from one-fourteenth of 20 down
31 Baker's dozen
32 Multiply 12 by 44
33 Subtract yards in a mile from 1 down
34 Add 5 across to 11 across

DOWN

1   Inches in 641 hands
2   Cube 61
4   Subtract 7 from 10 times 7 across
5   Minutes in 3 days
6   Add cube of 8 to cube of 9
9   Square of 1 down
10 Seven-ninths of 5,360,418
12 Ounces in 185 pounds

Answer on page 485

15 Subtract half a dozen from triple 18 down

17 Multiply Snow White's dwarfs by 4 down

18 Add 1 across to one-fifth of 2,035

19 Subtract 1 down from 14 across

20 Multiply 28 across by 3 across

23 Days in 27 leap years

24 319 dozen

26 Square feet in 113 square yards

29 Yards in 5 chains

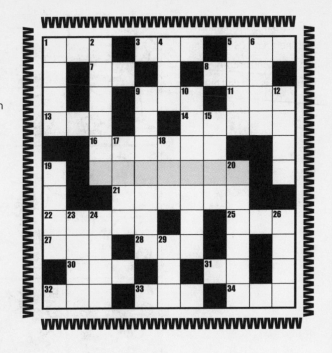

There are four pairs of mirror images here. Can you work out which ones they are, and which figure is the odd one out?

Answer on page 485

Calculate the price of each envelope, bottle of glue, pencil, and roll of tape.

Answer on page 485

Four students were playing bridge at a table in the corner of the student union building at college. From the clues given below, can you fully identify the player in each of the four seats, and name the subject she is majoring in?

Clues

1 The player in the North seat is studying for a degree in engineering.

2 Karen, the law student, is partnered by Ruff.

3 Amanda Hart is in the seat 90 degrees counterclockwise from the theology student.

4 The medical student, Shuffell, is not Petra.

First names: Amanda; Josephine; Karen; Petra
Surnames: Diamond; Hart; Ruff; Shuffell
Subjects: engineering; law; medicine; theology

Starting tip: Begin by naming the subject studied by Amanda Hart.

First name: _____
Surname: _____
Subject: _____

First name: _____
Surname: _____
Subject: _____

N

E

First name: _____
Surname: _____
Subject: _____

W

S

First name: _____
Surname: _____
Subject: _____

Answer on page 485

Place a number from 1 to 9 in each empty square so that each row, each column, and each 3x3 block contains all the numbers from 1 to 9.

4								8
				7				
6			9		3			1
		1	2		7	3		
	4		8		9		6	
	7			8			5	
	6	3	4		1	8	2	
2	8						1	4

Answer on page 485

Can you spot ten differences between these two sledding pictures?

Answer on page 486

178 · STRAPPED

The six straps leading from the central hexagon each contain three different instances of the numbers 1 to 18. From the clues given below, can you place each number in the correct position on the correct strap?

Clues

1 The six innermost numbers total 64.

2 The single-digit middle number on strap A minus the number outside it produces the outermost number on strap F.

3 There are just two even numbers, one of which is the outermost one, on strap E, but only one on strap F.

4 5 is the innermost number on strap D; the 7 is not on the strap directly opposite.

5 17 and 12 are separated by the 1 on one of the straps.

6 The 10 on one strap, which is immediately next to the 16, is in the same relative position as the 3 on another, but the 6 is farther away from the center than the 15 on an adjacent strap.

7 Strap C, which has only one two-digit number on it, does not contain the 1 or 2. The 2 corresponds in its position with the 13 on another strap.

8 The largest of the three numbers on strap B is not its innermost one; the outermost one is a lower number than the innermost number of the strap opposite, which is ten higher than the corresponding number on strap F.

Starting tip:
Start by working out which is the strap referred to in clue 5.

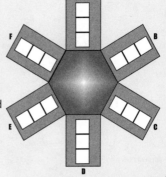

Answer on page 486

179 · DISCARD

Remove 35 cards by eliminating each of the following seven "hands" of five cards, leaving one card. For each hand, none of the five cards you select must be in the same row or column as any of the others. So which is the discard?

Straight flush: five cards in sequence from the same suit.
(ace high.)
Four of a kind and a ten.
Straight: five cards in sequence, any suits.
Flush: any five cards of the same suit, not all in sequence.
Full house: three of one kind and two of another kind.
Two pair of the same kind and a seven.
Two pair of the same kind and a ten, total value 38.
(ace = 1, king = 13.)

Card Checklist

	6	7	8	9	10	J	Q	K	A
CLUBS									
DIAMONDS									
HEARTS									
SPADES									

Answer on page 487

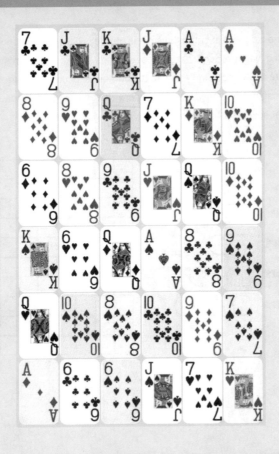

180 · BATTLESHIPS

Do you remember the old game of battleships? This puzzle is based on that idea. Your task is to find the vessels in the diagram. Some parts of boats or sea squares have already been filled in, and a number next to a row or column refers to the number of occupied squares in that row or column. The boats may be positioned horizontally or vertically, but no two boats or parts of boats are in adjacent squares—horizontally, vertically, or diagonally.

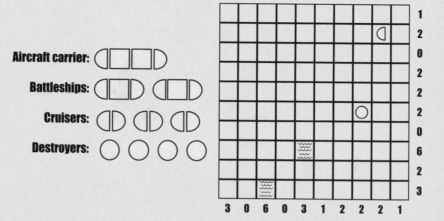

Aircraft carrier:

Battleships:

Cruisers:

Destroyers:

Answer on page 487

181 · HIDE AND SEEK

Four of the six objects lined up at the top are hidden in the picture. Can you see which ones and where they are?

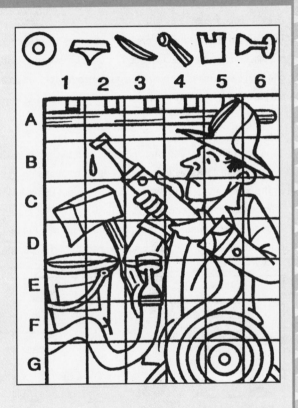

Answer on page 487

182 · ON THE GREEN

The diagram shows four players involved in a game of lawn bowling. Each has had one shot, and the player numbered 1 is just about to bowl his second wood. From the clues given below, can you fully identify all four players, and work out what headgear each is wearing (or, in one case, not) to protect him from the hot sun?

Clues

1 As you look at the diagram, Charles is next farther down the green from Jacks, who is wearing the straw boater.

2 The bareheaded player, whose surname is not Byass, is in position 3.

3 Walter is not player number 2.

4 James, who is wearing the floppy sunhat, is not number 1, the player about to bowl his next wood, whose surname is Green.

First names: Charles; Donald; James; Walter
Surnames: Byass; Green; Jacks; Wood
Headgear: bareheaded; baseball cap; floppy sunhat; straw boater

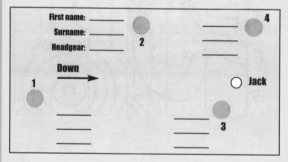

Starting tip: Begin by working out what player 1 is wearing on his head.

Answer on page 487

The professor is looking for four identical artifacts. Which will he choose?

Answer on page 487

Follow the dots to find what's fascinating Stanley!

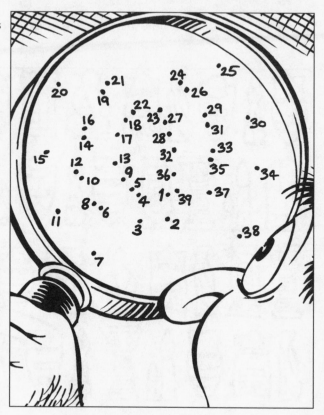

Answer on page 487

185 · PILE UP

These piles of blocks aren't the random results of a child playing but clues to a final, at present blank, pile on the right. Like the rest, that one has six blocks each with a different one of the six letters. The numbers below the heaps tell you two things:

(a) The number of adjacent pairs of blocks in that column which also appear adjacent in the final pile.

(b) The number of adjacent pairs of blocks that make a correct pair but the wrong way up.

So: 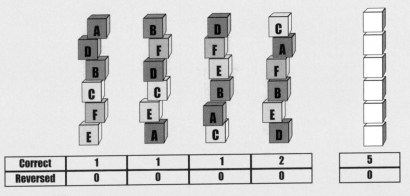 would score one in the "Correct" row if the final heap had an A directly above a C and one in the "Reversed" row if the final heap had a C on top of an A. From all this, can you create the final pile before it topples?

Correct	1	1	1	2		5
Reversed	0	0	0	0		0

Answer on page 487

186 · LOGI-PATH

Use your deductive reasoning to form a pathway from START to FINISH moving either horizontally or vertically (but not diagonally). The number at the beginning of every row or column indicates exactly how many boxes in that row or column your pathway must pass through. The small diagram is given as an example of how it works.

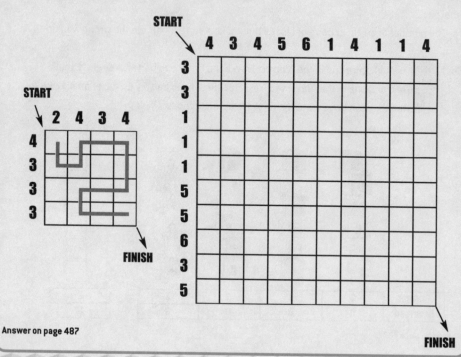

Answer on page 487

187 · IDENTICAL TWINS

Have a look at these eight unfortunate victims of the plague. Two of these poor creatures are as sick as each other. Can you find the two identical pictures?

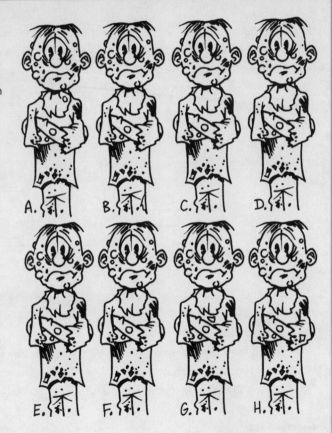

Answer on page 487

188 · NO BIG DEAL

Four cards were dealt face up on the table by four friends about to draw for partners. By chance, each card dealt was of a different value and a different suit. From the clues given below, can you say who dealt each of cards 1 to 4, and identify each card?

Players: Andrew; Bevis;
Charlie; Dean
Values: 2; 5; 8; jack
Suits: clubs; diamonds;
hearts; spades

	1	2	3	4
Player:	_____	_____	_____	_____
Value:	_____	_____	_____	_____
Suit:	_____	_____	_____	_____

Starting tip: Begin by working out the value of the heart.

Clues

1 The card dealt by Bevis was of a higher value than the heart, which is somewhere to the left of the 8 in the layout.

2 Dean's card was a diamond.

3 One card was the 5 of clubs, which is farther left on the table than the spade.

4 Charlie's card was a higher one than card 2.

5 The card dealt by Andrew is two places to the right of the jack in the deal.

Answer on page 488

189 · BATTLESHIPS

Do you remember the old game of battleships? This puzzle is based on that idea. Your task is to find the vessels in the diagram. Some parts of boats or sea squares have already been filled in, and a number next to a row or column refers to the number of occupied squares in that row or column. The boats may be positioned horizontally or vertically, but no two boats or parts of boats are in adjacent squares—horizontally, vertically, or diagonally.

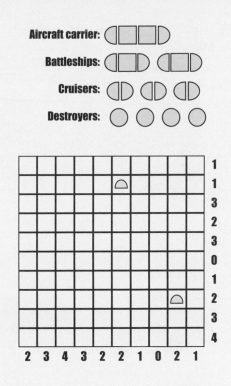

Aircraft carrier:
Battleships:
Cruisers:
Destroyers:

1
1
3
2
3
0
1
2
3
4

2 3 4 3 2 2 1 0 2 1

Answer on page 488

190 · FRAMED!

The top illustration shows four abstract paintings hanging in a famous art gallery. Below, we see Claud, who has bought one—but he can't remember which it was or which way up it should hang. Can you help him?

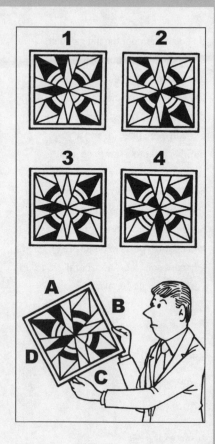

Answer on page 488

Trust Annie to make anything but a normal snowman. Follow the dots to see her creation.

Answer on page 488

Four of the six objects shown at the top can be found in the larger picture. Can you see which ones and where they are?

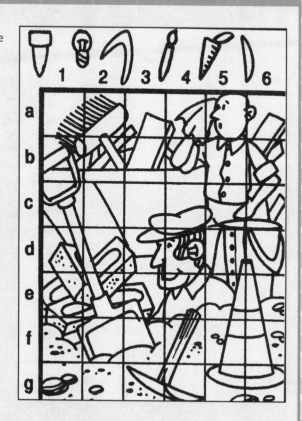

Answer on page 488

193 · WIRED UP

Which one of the four plugs will connect the washing machine to the electricity?

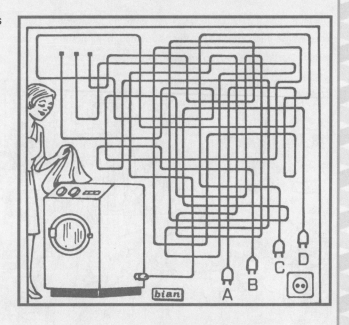

bian

A
B
C
D

Answer on page 488

The picture on the right was taken only a few minutes after the one on the left. In that time, ten people have been into various shops and bought something—some are even wearing their purchases. Who are the ten shoppers and what have they bought?

Answer on page 488

195 · BATTLESHIPS

Do you remember the old game of battleships? This puzzle is based on that idea. Your task is to find the vessels in the diagram. Some parts of boats or sea squares have already been filled in, and a number next to a row or column refers to the number of occupied squares in that row or column. The boats may be positioned horizontally or vertically, but no two boats or parts of boats are in adjacent squares— horizontally, vertically, or diagonally.

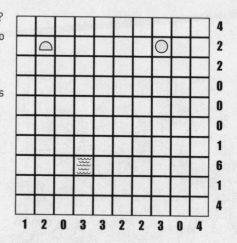

Aircraft carrier:

Battleships:

Cruisers:

Destroyers:

Answer on page 488

Place a number from 1 to 9 in each empty square so that each row, each column, and each 3x3 block contains all the numbers from 1 to 9.

8		6				9		4
	3						2	
		4	6	3	2	1		
3			4		5			1
			3		8			
9			2		1			7
		3	1	2	4	8		
	7						1	
1		9				4		2

Answer on page 489

197 · ABC

Each line, across and down, should contain each of the letters A, B, and C, and two empty squares. The letter outside the grid shows the first or second letter in the direction of the arrow. Can you fill in the grid?

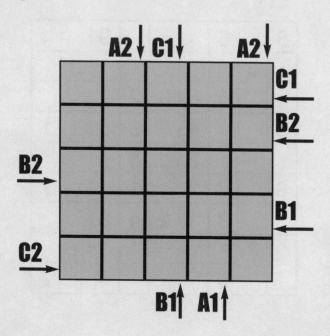

Answer on page 489

198 · LATIN SQUARE

The grid is to be filled in with numbers from 1 to 6 so that each number appears exactly once in each row and each column. The clues refer to the digit totals in the squares mentioned. For example, DEF2=9 would mean that the numbers in D2, E2, and F2 add up to 9.

A456=10 CDE6=14
AB2=5 D345=7
B123=14 E12=7
C123=7 EF4=10
CDE3=6 F123=8

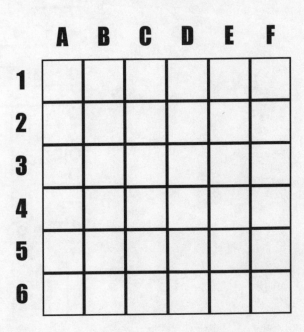

Answer on page 489

199 · MAZE-WAYS

Each obstacle along the path carries a penalty as shown in the key in the middle. Can you travel from A to B while incurring a total of 40 penalty points?

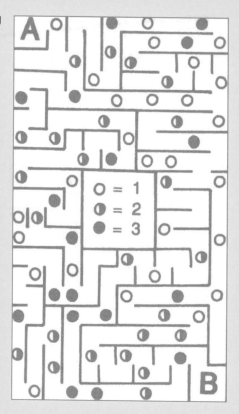

O = 1
◑ = 2
● = 3

Answer on page 489

Our distracted artist has made five mistakes while drawing this picture. Can you spot them?

Answer on page 489

201 · SNACK TIME

As Tommy walked down the street he met in fairly quick succession four of his friends, each of whom was eating something different. As it was a rather chilly day, each boy was wearing a sweater. From the clues given (right), can you name each of the boys numbered 1 to 4 in the diagram in the order in which they were met, say what color sweater each was wearing, and what item each was eating?

Clues

1 Tommy met Kevin, who was wearing the blue sweater, some time later than he came across the boy who was eating a lollipop.

2 The boy in the beige sweater was the third friend Tommy met.

3 The youth eating a banana, who was not Simon, was encountered right after the one wearing the green sweater.

4 The boy in the red sweater, who was not Danny, was encountered some time after Lewis, whose snack was the chocolate bar.

Answer on page 489

Names: Danny; Kevin; Lewis; Simon
Sweaters: beige; blue; green; red
Snacks: apple; banana; chocolate bar; lollipop

Starting tip: First name the boy in the red sweater.

Tommy

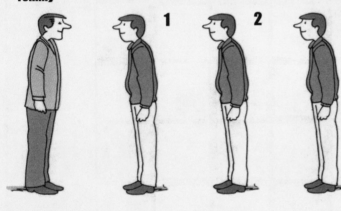

Name: _____   _____   _____   _____

Sweater: _____   _____   _____   _____

Snack: _____   _____   _____   _____

202 · LOGI-5

Each line, across and down, is to have each of the letters A, B, C, D, and E, appearing once each. Also, every shape—shown by the thick lines—must have each of the letters in it. Can you fill in the grid?

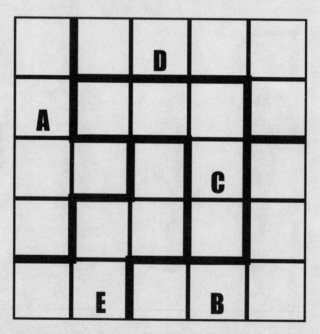

Answer on page 489

203 · PAINT BOX

Arthur has started a painting, but he has gotten his paintbrushes muddled up. How many paintbrushes can you spot on this page?

Answer on page 489

204 · BLOCKS AWAY

This puzzled archaeologist has realized that there will be three blocks missing if he tries to reconstruct the original mural shown at the top left. Which ones are they?

Answer on page 489

205 · MINIMAZE

Each obstacle along the maze's path carries a penalty (as shown in the central box). See if you can find your way from A to B, while incurring a total of 40 penalty points.

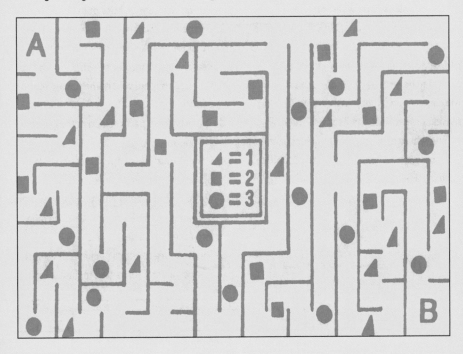

Answer on page 489

Since buying a metal detector, Derek has been taking every opportunity to search for buried valuables. Last week, he took his new toy out on five occasions, but took so long to find anything at all each time that he gave up in despair when the first item he dug up proved to be little better than rubbish. From the clues given (right), can you put Derek's five excursions into their correct order, saying where he went, how long he spent searching, and what he eventually found on each occasion?

Clues

1 The rusty doorknob turned up after a 20-minute search, but not in Derek's garden.

2 On the third occasion he used his metal detector, Derek spent over half an hour searching in a farmer's field, but it was not that day that he went home having found only a bottle top.

3 The trip to the park yielded nothing but an old spoon.

4 Derek's fourth attempt at locating hidden riches culminated in the discovery of a wrench after a search lasting for less than 40 minutes; the 25-minute hunt on a beach had taken place before this.

5 The treasure-hunter's second outing with his metal detector lasted for just 15 minutes.

Order	Place	Time spent	Item found

Answer on page 490

	Beach	Farmer's field	Friend's garden	Own garden	Park	15 minutes	20 minutes	25 minutes	35 minutes	40 minutes	Bottle top	Doorknob	Wrench	Spoon	Toy car
First															
Second															
Third															
Fourth															
Fifth															
Bottle top											
Doorknob											
Wrench											
Spoon											
Toy car											
15 minutes						
20 minutes						
25 minutes						
35 minutes						
40 minutes						

Record in this grid all the information obtained from the clues, by using a cross to indicate a definite "no" and a check to show a definite "yes." Transfer these to all sections of the grid thus eliminating all but one possibility, which must be the correct one.

207 · IT'S TRICKY

These rabbits are stumped! The numbers next to the grid show what the symbols in those rows or columns add up to. See if you can work out what number each symbol stands for, and what number should replace the question mark beneath the first column.

Answer on page 490

Each line, across and down, is to have each of the letters A, B, C, D, and E, appearing once each. Also, every shape—shown by the thick lines—must have each of the letters in it. Can you fill in the grid?

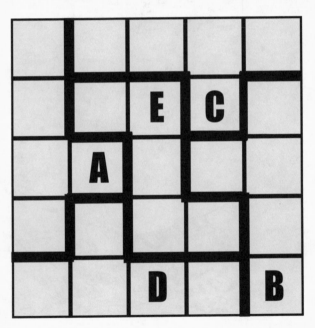

Answer on page 490

Follow the dots to find out why Rocky and the dinosaur are hiding underneath this rock.

Answer on page 490

210 · BATTLESHIPS

Do you remember the old game of battleships? This puzzle is based on that idea. Your task is to find the vessels in the diagram. Some parts of boats or sea squares have already been filled in, and a number next to a row or column refers to the number of occupied squares in that row or column. The boats may be positioned horizontally or vertically, but no two boats or parts of boats are in adjacent squares—horizontally, vertically, or diagonally.

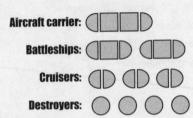

Aircraft carrier:
Battleships:
Cruisers:
Destroyers:

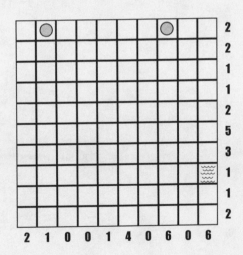

2
2
1
1
2
5
3
1
1
2

2 1 0 0 1 4 0 6 0 6

Answer on page 490

211 · BLOCKS AWAY

The archaeologist has found that there are three blocks missing when he tries to reconstruct the original mural shown in the top right-hand corner. Which ones are they?

Answer on page 490

212 · WHAT'S THE POINT?

Each number from 1 to 10 appears once in this star, either at a point or at an intersection. The numbers 2, 10, 5, and 3 appear in that order along a straight line. Number 1 is one of the numbers that is closer to the center and 9 is at one of the star's five points. Numbers 8 and 6 are at opposite ends of one of the lines, while 4 is the next number clockwise from 7 in the center. The numbers at A and D total 10, as do those at G and K. Number 10 is located higher than 1 but lower than 8. Where is each number?

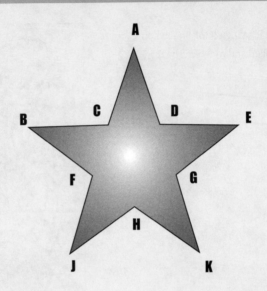

Answer on page 490

Which tangles will knot when
pulled and which will not?

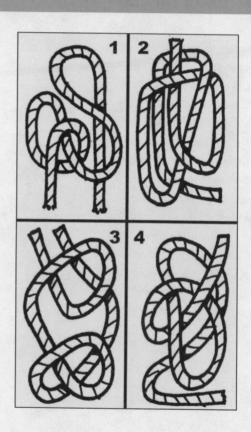

Answer on page 490

Each line, across and down, is to have each of the letters A, B, C, D, and E, appearing once each. Also, every shape—shown by the thick lines—must have each of the letters in it. Can you fill in the grid?

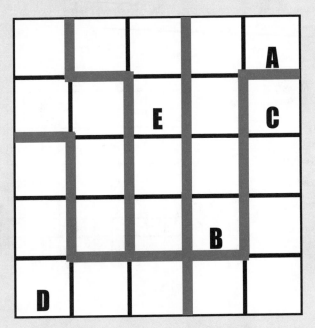

Answer on page 490

215 · BATTLESHIPS

Do you remember the old game of battleships? This puzzle is based on that idea. Your task is to find the vessels in the diagram. Some parts of boats or sea squares have already been filled in, and a number next to a row or column refers to the number of occupied squares in that row or column. The boats may be positioned horizontally or vertically, but no two boats or parts of boats are in adjacent squares—horizontally, vertically, or diagonally.

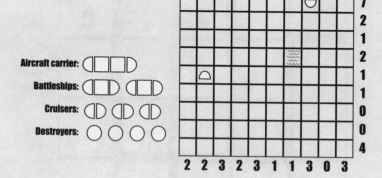

216 · NUMBER JIG

Fit the numbers into the grid as quickly as possible. One has been done for you.

2 figures
26
47
60
93

3 figures
229
307
480
549
738
816

4 figures
2049
3251
4788
5177
6074
7756
~~8352~~
9703

5 figures
39214
68644

7 figures
2148471
5739600

9 figures
285092204
330518140

Answer on page 490

217 · RED, WHITE, AND BLUE

Each cell of the square is colored red, white or blue. Each row, each column, and each of the two long diagonals contains exactly two cells of each color. The information in each clue refers only to the cells in that row or column. From the clues below, can you tell which color each cell is?

1 The reds are between the blues.
2 The whites are adjacent.
3 The whites are between the reds.
4 The blues are to the right of the reds.
5 No two squares of the same color are adjacent.
6 The blues are between the whites.

A The blues are adjacent.
B Each white is immediately above a blue.
C No two squares of the same color are adjacent.
D The whites are above the reds.
E The whites are above the blues.
F The reds are above the whites.

Answer on page 490

218 · FAMILY TREE

Using the family tree, can you answer the following questions?

1 What is Sally and Andrew's unmarried daughter called?
2 What relation is Victor to Beth?
3 Which couple has the most children?
4 What relation is Billy to Simon?
5 What is Andy's relation to the person he's named after?
6 How many grandchildren do Sally and Andrew have?
7 Which couple has two children?

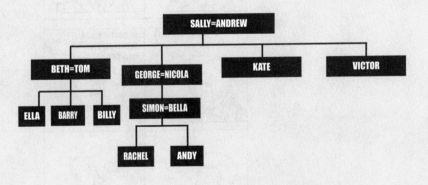

Answer on page 491

219 · WHO'S WHO?

Can you match each doctor to his patient?

Answer on page 491

220 · NUMBER JIG

Fit the numbers into the grid as quickly as possible. One has been done for you.

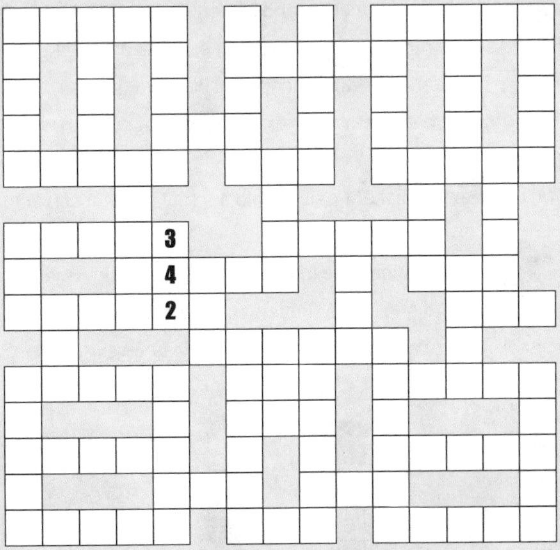

3 figures
237
~~342~~
402
418
451
513
625
686
705
748
814
950
974
988

4 figures
1358
2369
3743
5606

5 figures
14268
16999
20294
23776
25358
35010
39092
41636
41892
43914
50326
50371
51169
52049
54102
59322
61505
62008
62259
71703
75882
81556
81655
83199
89093
93721
99206

6 figures
138261
283863
659144
764132
841023

Answer on page 491

221 · PILE UP

These piles of blocks aren't the random results of a child playing but clues to a final, at present blank, pile on the right. Like the rest, that one has six blocks each with a different one of the six letters. The numbers below the heaps tell you two things:

(a) The number of adjacent pairs of blocks in that column which also appear adjacent in the final pile.

(b) The number of adjacent pairs of blocks that make a correct pair but the wrong way up.

So: would score one in the "Correct" row if the final heap had an A directly above a C and one in the "Reversed" row if the final heap had a C on top of an A. From all this, can you create the final pile before it topples?

Correct	0	0	0	1		5
Reversed	2	2	0	0		0

Answer on page 491

Calculate the price of each pen, pencil, ruler, and bottle of ink.

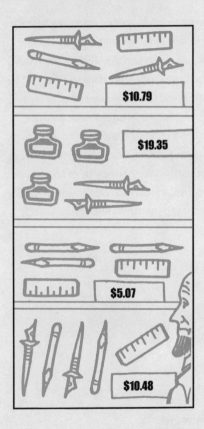

Answer on page 491

I bought a parrot recently, intending to teach him to talk. Unfortunately, it seemed that someone had gotten there before me. I had five visitors on different days last week—two relatives and three men who came to repair things—and the parrot responded to their courteous greetings extremely rudely. From the clues given here, can you work out when each visitor called and how he or she greeted my parrot, and can you also decide what rude response the parrot came out with in each case?

Clues

1 The man who came to the house on Wednesday greeted the parrot with a chirpy "Good morning." The carpenter's visit took place the following day.

2 "Get out of here!" was the bird's response to the person who said, "Nice to meet you."

3 The TV repairman was not the person the parrot told to "Buzz off!"

4 The plumber greeted my pet by saying "Hello"; he was not my Tuesday visitor, who was told by the parrot to "Get lost!"

5 My sister, who did not visit on Monday, spoke her greeting with a friendly smile, and was taken aback when the bird responded with a curt "Go away!"

6 Friday's visitor was not the person whose words to the parrot were "Who's a pretty boy?"

Answer on page 491

Record in this grid all the information obtained from the clues, by using a cross to indicate a definite "no" and a check to show a definite "yes." Transfer these to all sections of the grid thus eliminating all but one possibility, which must be the correct one.

Day	Visitor	Greeting	Response

224 · LOGI-PATH

Use your deductive reasoning to form a pathway from START to FINISH moving either horizontally or vertically (but not diagonally). The number at the beginning of every row or column indicates exactly how many boxes in that row or column your pathway must pass through. The small diagram is given as an example of how it works.

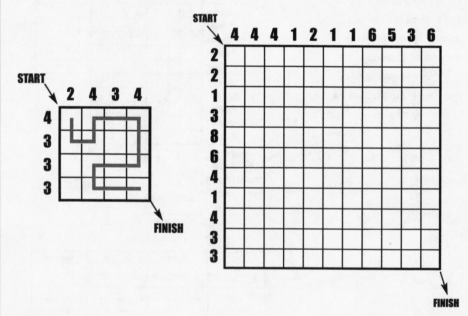

Answer on page 491

Shade in every fragment containing a dot—and what have you got?

Answer on page 491

226 · ABC

Each line, across and down, should contain each of the letters A, B, and C, and two empty squares. The letter outside the grid shows the first or second letter in the direction of the arrow. Can you fill in the grid?

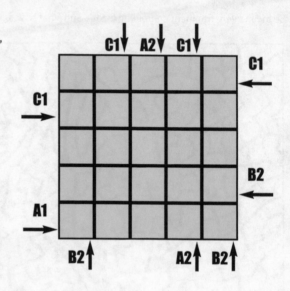

Answer on page 491

227 · SQUARE LETTERS

The letters of the alphabet, excluding Z, are entered into a 5 x 5 square so that no two consecutive letters are in the same row or column, or in a diagonal in any direction. The letters NQG can be read downward as can TMO. Square E5 is a vowel. D is immediately left of V and immediately above I, which is not in column 2. Row D begins and ends with a vowel, the first alphabetically preceding the latter. Q and T are at opposite ends of a row, and K and S are at the top and bottom respectively of a column. U is diagonally just below W; E and R can both be seen on the same long diagonal. C is diagonally adjacent to H; Y is to the immediate right of F, and X is in a corner square.

Can you locate each letter?

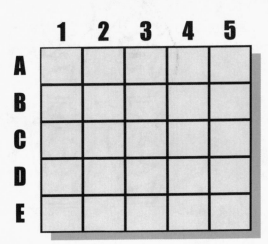

Answer on page 491

228 · FOURSOME

Which four of the twelve vases are identical?

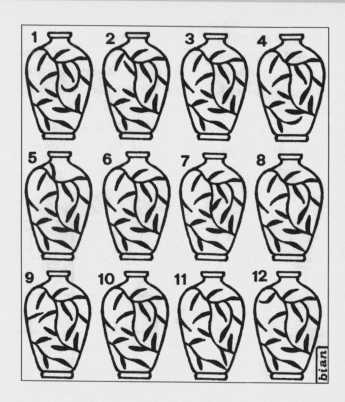

Answer on page 491

229 · TANGLED TAPE

Trevor sent four videos to the *Falldownlaughing* show but only one was accepted. Follow the tangled tape from the film. The correct film will finish at Trev's camcorder.

GRAN FALLING OFF A CHAIR

DAD FALLING OFF A LADDER

MUM FALLING IN THE FISH POND

LITTLE SISTER FALLS OUT OF BED

Answer on page 491

230 · DOMINO SEARCH

A standard set of dominoes has been laid out, using numbers instead of dots for clarity. Using a sharp pencil and a keen brain, can you draw in the lines to show where each domino has been placed? You may find the check grid useful—crossing off each domino as you find it.

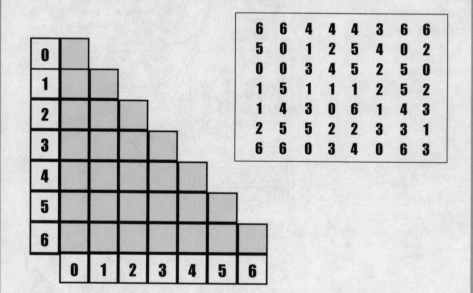

Answer on page 491

231 · COG-ITATE

When the handle is turned in the direction shown, which two of the four weights will rise and which two will fall?

Answer on page 492

232 · WIRED UP

Which plug should be inserted in the socket in order for the lamp to work?

Answer on page 492

233 · TWINNED UP

This woman would like to buy a pair of matching vases. Can you help her choose two identical vases?

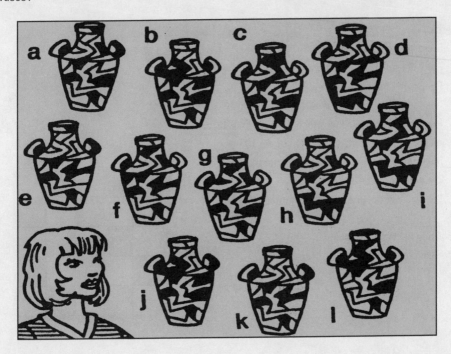

Answer on page 492

234 · UNLUCKY FOR SOME

Each of the white squares in the diagram contains a different one of the numbers 1 to 13. From the clues given below, can you place the correct number in each of the squares?

Clues

1 There are no two-digit numbers in rows A or D, or in columns 1 or 4.

2 The 9 does not occupy a corner square.

3 The 6 is in direct line below the 2.

4 The number in E5 is one less than the one in A3.

5 The 1 is diagonally below and to the left of the 12, and diagonally above and to the right of the 10.

6 The number in square B4 is two higher than the one in square D2.

7 The 8 is in direct line above the number 13.

Starting tip: Start by placing the 1 in its correct position.

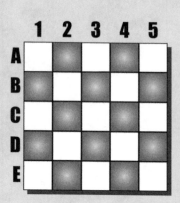

Answer on page 492

Four of the six objects shown at the top are hidden in the picture. Which ones are they and in which squares do they appear?

Answer on page 492

Arrange the dominoes so that the spots at both ends of each arrow are the same, as they would be in a normal game. We've entered the 0–6 to get you started.

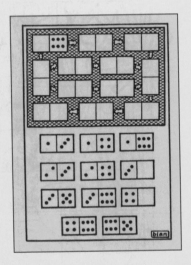

Answer on page 492

Which two numbered fragments complete either wheel A or wheel B?

Answer on page 492

238 · SILHOUETTE

Shade in every fragment containing a dot—and what have you got?

Answer on page 492

In the picture on the left, the man is selecting a suitcase. In the right-hand picture, he has made his choice. Which did he choose?

Answer on page 492

240 · ZEROING IN

Twenty of the twenty-five squares in the diagram each contain a different one of the numbers 1 to 20; each of the other five squares contains a zero. From the clues given below, can you place the correct number in each square? Note: The term "number" or "single-digit number" does not include zeros.

Clues

1 No row, column, or diagonal (long or short) contains more than one zero.
2 The 19 in square B3 is the only two-digit number in that row; the 7 is the only single-digit number in row 2.
3 The 9 is immediately below the 16, and immediately left of the 12.
4 The numbers in column E total 45, and those in row 2 total 51.
5 The number in A4 is five higher than the one in E5, which is itself one higher than the one in C2.
6 The 11 is immediately to the right of the 5 in row 4; the 2 is in a higher row than the 4.
7 The 17 appears in column D, somewhere below a zero and somewhere above the 8.
8 The four numbers in column C are all even numbers, but do not include the 18.
9 The number 1 can be found in row 5, and the 6 in row 1.
10 The 10 is in the same column as the 3, but higher up.

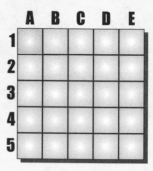

Starting tip: Begin by placing the 9.

Answer on page 492

241 · ON THE MARKET

The large picture has been reproduced underneath in twelve pieces. However, three of the pieces contain an extra detail, while four pieces have a detail missing. Can you spot all the extra and missing details?

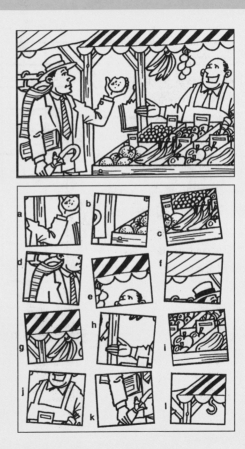

Answer on page 493

242 · BATTLESHIPS

Do you remember the old game of battleships? This puzzle is based on that idea. Your task is to find the vessels in the diagram. Some parts of boats or sea squares have already been filled in, and a number next to a row or column refers to the number of occupied squares in that row or column. The boats may be positioned horizontally or vertically, but no two boats or parts of boats are in adjacent squares—horizontally, vertically, or diagonally.

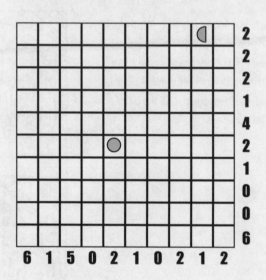

Aircraft carrier:
Battleships:
Cruisers:
Destroyers:

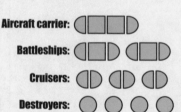

Answer on page 493

243 · SQUARE NUMBERS

The numbers 1–25 are entered randomly in a 5 x 5 square so that no two consecutive numbers are adjacent in any direction, or in the same row or column.

Column 1 contains four multiples of 5, but not 20, which is in the same row as 5. C3 is one lower than A2, which is four lower than B1, which is one higher than E2, which is one higher than A3, which is a prime number. B4 plus D3 equals D5; E3 plus A5, which are consecutive numbers, equals A4; C2 is an even number. B3, which is one higher than E4, is twice C4; B5 is a multiple of C5, which is not 1. Number 7 is in the same line diagonally as 8, and 6 is immediately below an even number; 8 is below an odd number. Number 22 is below and diagonally adjacent to 2, which is in the same row as 14. If the long diagonal from top left to bottom right contains only one odd number, can you complete the grid?

	1	2	3	4	5
A					
B					
C					
D					
E					

Answer on page 493

244 · LOGI-5

Each line, across and down, is to have each of the letters A, B, C, D, and E, appearing once each. Also, every shape—shown by the thick lines —must have each of the letters in it. Can you fill in the grid?

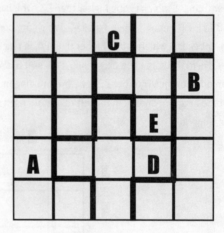

Answer on page 493

245 · ENSIGN

Starting from 9, find one way by which—if you insert all four arithmetical signs (two of them twice) in the blank squares and carry out all the operations in sequence—you can obtain the answer 6 (as shown).

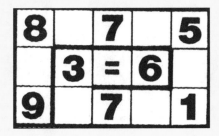

Answer on page 493

246 · TELL-ING DETAILS

Each picture is lacking in one detail that is present in the other seven. What are those details?

Answer on page 493

247 · STAR STUDENTS

In a magazine article, three popular Albion TV personalities talk about their time at college, studying for careers that they never pursued after getting into television. From the clues given (right), can you work out each woman's full name, what she does on Albion TV, and what she trained to be originally?

Clues

1. It wasn't Donna who was trained as a teacher.
2. Miss Knight is host of Albion TV's popular Saturday evening quiz show *Go For It!*
3. Laura is a news anchor, presenting Albion TV's flagship 9:00 p.m. news summary every weekday.
4. Susan Niven never had any ambition to be a nurse.
5. It isn't the one-time student teacher who now presents current affairs programs for Albion TV.

Answer on page 494

	Knight	Niven	Robins	News anchor	Current affairs host	Quiz show host	Nurse	Lawyer	Teacher
Donna									
Laura									
Susan									
Nurse									
Lawyer									
Teacher									
News anchor									
Current affairs host									
Quiz show host									

First name	Surname	TV career	Studied as

There are eight differences
between the two cartoons.
Can you spot them?

Answer on page 494

249 · SUDOKU

Place a number from 1 to 9 in each empty square so that each row, each column, and each 3x3 block contains all the numbers from 1 to 9.

2			3		1	7		
			9			1	3	
8						6		9
	8	2		6				
					2			
	4	1		9				
3						4		8
			5			9	2	
6			1		9	3		

Answer on page 494

250 · BATTLESHIPS

Do you remember the old game of battleships? This puzzle is based on that idea. Your task is to find the vessels in the diagram. Some parts of boats or sea squares have already been filled in, and a number next to a row or column refers to the number of occupied squares in that row or column. The boats may be positioned horizontally or vertically, but no two boats or parts of boats are in adjacent squares—horizontally, vertically, or diagonally.

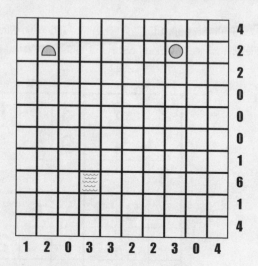

Aircraft carrier:

Battleships:

Cruisers:

Destroyers:

Answer on page 494

251 · FITBITS

The shoppers are enjoying the last minute rush at a sale. Can you work out which two of the five details on the left belong to two of the bargain-hunters?

Answer on page 494

252 · PILE UP

These piles of blocks aren't the random results of a child playing but clues to a final, at present blank, pile on the right. Like the rest, that one has six blocks each with a different one of the six letters. The numbers below the heaps tell you two things:

(a) The number of adjacent pairs of blocks in that column which also appear adjacent in the final pile.

(b) The number of adjacent pairs of blocks that make a correct pair but the wrong way up.

So: would score one in the "Correct" row if the final heap had an A directly above a C and one in the "Reversed" row if the final heap had a C on top of an A. From all this, can you create the final pile before it topples?

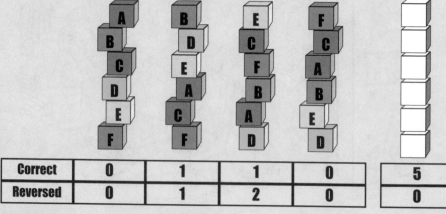

Correct	0	1	1	0	5
Reversed	0	1	2	0	0

Answer on page 494

253 · LEAF DIVISION

Without lifting your pen or pencil from the page, draw a continuous line to divide the clover leaf into four sections, each containing six different shapes.

Answer on page 494

254 · MATCH UP

Can you see which two boxes contain the same four symbols?

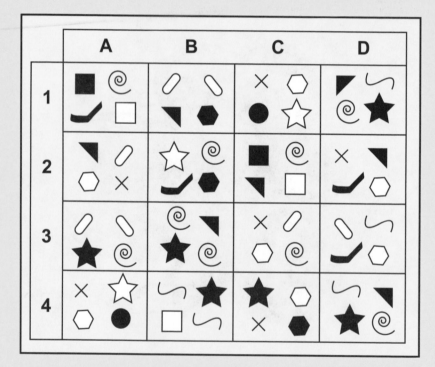

Answer on page 494

A square has sides of equal length. How many squares of all sizes are more red than green?

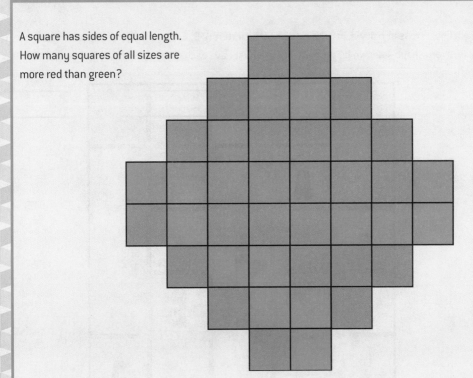

Answer on page 494

256 · LOGI-5

Each line, across and down, is to have each of the letters A, B, C, D, and E, appearing once each. Also, every shape—shown by the thick lines—must have each of the letters in it. Can you fill in the grid?

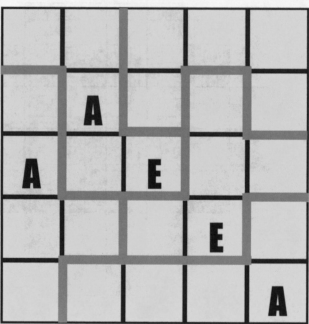

Answer on page 494

257 · MATCH UP

Can you see which two boxes contain the same four symbols?

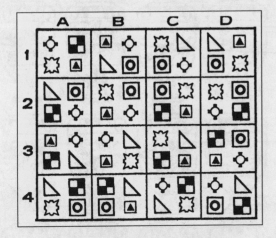

Answer on page 494

258 · FOURSOME

Which four of the twelve vases are identical?

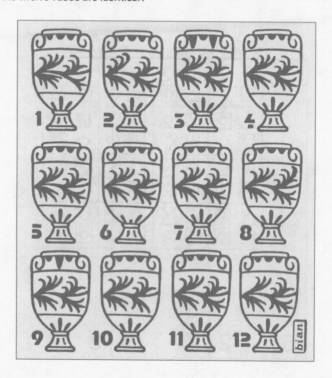

Answer on page 494

Place a number from 1 to 9 in each empty square so that each row, each column, and each 3x3 block contains all the numbers from 1 to 9.

				5				
		3	4		6	1		
	7						3	
		6	1		2	9		
		1		8		7		
	4						2	
7								2
			8		1			
6		2	7		5	8		4

Answer on page 495

Four of the six shapes shown at the top can be found hidden in the picture. Which ones and where are they?

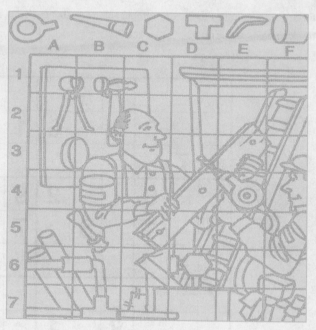

Answer on page 495

261 · DOMINO SEARCH

A standard set of dominoes has been laid out, using numbers instead of dots for clarity. Using a sharp pencil and a keen brain, can you draw in the lines to show where each domino has been placed? You may find the check grid useful—crossing off each domino as you find it. To give you a start, 3–5 has been marked in.

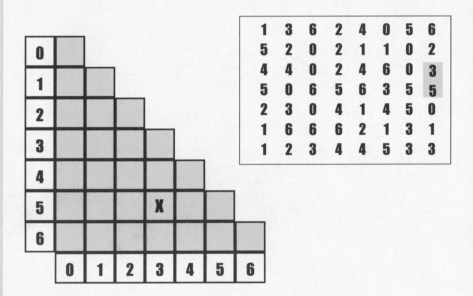

262 · CAN YOU DIGIT?

ACROSS

1 (6 across plus 11 down) squared
6 11 across reversed minus five
7 Square number
8 (6 across times three, plus 4 down reversed) squared
9 2 down minus seven
11 First two digits of 5 down
12 (10 down minus one) cubed

DOWN

1 (2nd, 3rd, and 4th digits of 1 across reversed) squared
2 (4 down minus one) reversed
3 (9 across reversed plus one) cubed, minus four
4 One-third of (9 across reversed)
5 Palindromic square
10 7 across minus two
11 No clue required

1	2	3	4	5
6			7	
8				
9	10		11	
12				

Answer on page 495

263 · ABC

Each line, across and down, should contain each of the letters A, B, and C, and two empty squares. The letter outside the grid shows the first or second letter in the direction of the arrow. Can you fill in the grid?

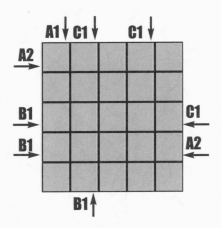

Answer on page 495

264 · SILHOUETTE

Shade every shape that contains a dot to reveal a scary creature.

Answer on page 495

265 · LOGI-PATH

Use your deductive reasoning to form a pathway from START to FINISH moving either horizontally or vertically (but not diagonally). The number at the beginning of every row or column indicates exactly how many boxes in that row or column your pathway must pass through. The small diagram is given as an example of how it works.

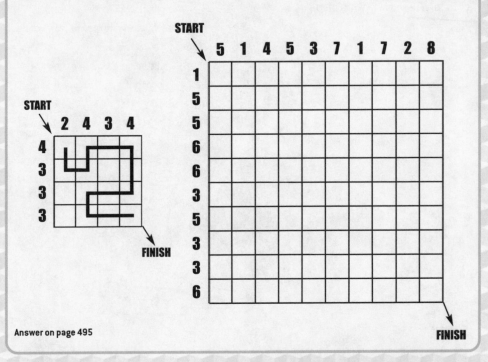

Answer on page 495

293

266 · STAMPS OF VALUE

A new set of stamps has just been issued in Philatelia, and four of the values are shown here. From the clues given (right), can you work out the design on each stamp, its face value, and the color in which its figures of value are printed?

Clues

1 The figure 5 does not appear in brown on any of the four stamps.

2 The stamp depicting the cathedral, which has a zero in its value panel, is shown immediately to the right of the brown stamp.

3 Stamp 4 has a 1 in its value panel; the harbor is not the design featured on stamp 3.

4 The 15 cents stamp is shown in a position directly above or below the blue one.

5 The red stamp bears the next highest value to that depicting the mountains, which is not in position 1.

Answer on page 495

Designs: cathedral; harbor; mountains; waterfall
Values: 10 cents; 15 cents; 25 cents; 50 cents
Colors: blue; brown; green; red

Starting tip: Begin by working out the value on the brown stamp.

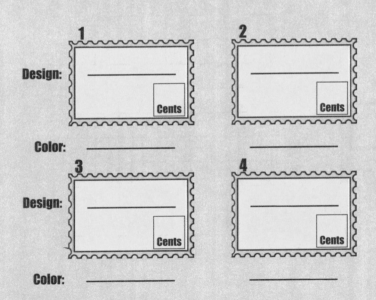

Design: _____ (1)   _____ (2)

Cents

Color: _____   _____

Design: _____ (3)   _____ (4)

Cents

Color: _____   _____

267 · LOGI-PATH

Use your deductive reasoning to form a pathway from START to FINISH moving either horizontally or vertically (but not diagonally). The number at the beginning of every row or column indicates exactly how many boxes in that row or column your pathway must pass through. The small diagram is given as an example of how it works.

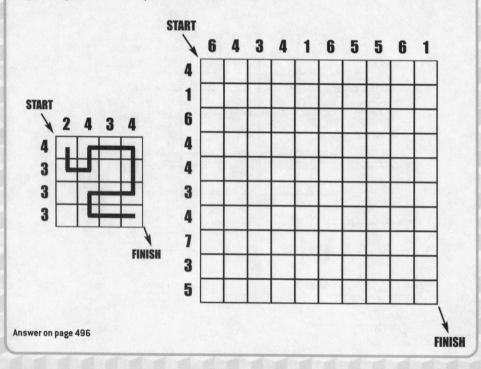

Answer on page 496

Each line, across and down, should contain each of the letters A, B, and C, and two empty squares. The letter outside the grid shows the first or second letter in the direction of the arrow. Can you fill in the grid?

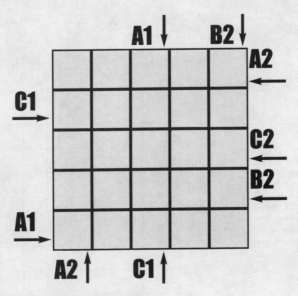

269 · PYRAMID

Which one of the numbered pieces of paper will, when folded, combine with the four-sided base at the top left to form a pyramid?

Answer on page 496

270 · BATTLESHIPS

Do you remember the old game of battleships? This puzzle is based on that idea. Your task is to find the vessels in the diagram. Some parts of boats or sea squares have already been filled in, and a number next to a row or column refers to the number of occupied squares in that row or column. The boats may be positioned horizontally or vertically, but no two boats or parts of boats are in adjacent squares—horizontally, vertically, or diagonally.

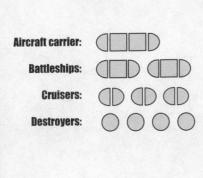

Aircraft carrier:

Battleships:

Cruisers:

Destroyers:

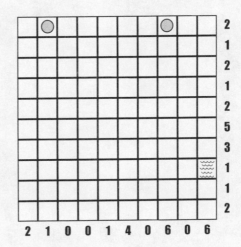

Answer on page 496

271 · TROUBLESOME TRIANGLE

The numbers 1–15 are to be inserted into the grid. No two consecutive numbers should be in the same row, arrowed diagonal, or diagonally adjacent box. The numbers on the left show the total in the horizontal row and those below show the total of the diagonal. Given that the numbers in the right-hand diagonal totaling 34 are all odd numbers, can you complete the grid?

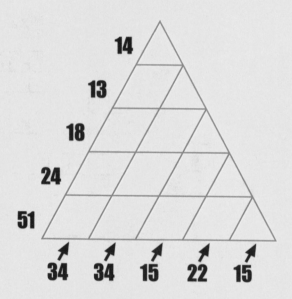

Answer on page 496

272 · DOMINO SEARCH

A standard set of dominoes has been laid out, using numbers instead of dots for clarity. Using a sharp pencil and a keen brain, can you draw in the lines to show where each domino has been placed? You may find the check grid useful—crossing off each domino as you find it.

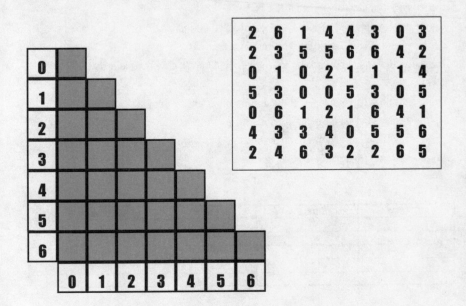

2	6	1	4	4	3	0	3
2	3	5	5	6	6	4	2
0	1	0	2	1	1	1	4
5	3	0	0	5	3	0	5
0	6	1	2	1	6	4	1
4	3	3	4	0	5	5	6
2	4	6	3	2	2	6	5

Answer on page 496

273 · LOGISTICAL

Five men have been employed in different capacities at the airport for varying lengths of time. What is each man's full name, what does he do, and for how many years has he worked at the airport?

Clues

1 The baggage handler joined the airport staff six years ago.

2 The electrician's period of service is longer than Ledger's.

3 It is five years since Quentin started work at the airport.

4 The traffic controller has worked there longer than Denzil, but not as long as Marshall.

5 Forrest has not been employed at the airport for as long as Banks.

6 Matthew enjoys his job as an airport security guard.

7 Lawrence Adamson has not worked at the airport for as long as the man whose voice is regularly heard on the public address system.

First name	Surname	Job	Length of service

Answer on page 496

	Adamson	Banks	Forrest	Ledger	Marshall	Announcer	Baggage handler	Electrician	Security guard	Traffic controller	4 years	5 years	6 years	7 years	8 years
Benedict															
Denzil															
Lawrence															
Matthew															
Quentin															
4 years															
5 years															
6 years															
7 years															
8 years															
Announcer															
Baggage handler															
Electrician															
Security guard															
Traffic controller															

Record in this grid all the information obtained from the clues, by using a cross to indicate a definite "no" and a check to show a definite "yes." Transfer these to all sections of the grid thus eliminating all but one possibility, which must be the correct one.

274 · THAT LITTLE BIT OF DIFFERENCE

There are eight differences between
the two cartoons. Can you spot them?

Answer on page 496

Untangle the lines to see who each musical instrument belongs to.

Answer on page 496

Which two of the boxes contain the same four symbols?

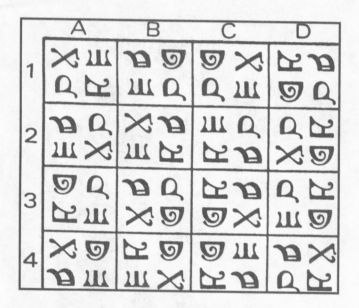

Answer on page 496

This astronaut seems to have lost her way! Can you guide her safely back to her spaceship?

Answer on page 496

Unfortunately, the DMV had to fail five drivers this morning. From the following information, can you discover the time of each candidate's test, the botched maneuver that contributed most to each failure, and where that maneuver took place?

Clues

1 Helen Weales messed up her reversing; Ron Gear came to grief in Hawthorn Way.

2 Roland Brake's test was at 9 o'clock, but his examiner didn't take him along Mill Road.

3 Rex Chance's test was an hour before that of the candidate who made a bad maneuver in Market Street, while Vera Swerve's test began half an hour after the one that was failed on the emergency stop.

4 The test failed on the parking maneuver began at 10:30.

5 The 9:30 candidate made a mistake in Balmoral Circle, and the failed hill start was halfway up Church Hill.

Time	Candidate	Maneuver	Location

Answer on page 497

	Roland Brake	Rex Chance	Ron Gear	Vera Swerve	Helen Weales	Emergency stop	Hill start	Parking	Reversing	Signaling	Balmoral Circle	Church Hill	Hawthorn Way	Market Street	Mill Road
9:00															
9:30															
10:30															
11:00															
11:30															
Balmoral Circle															
Church Hill															
Hawthorn Way															
Market Street															
Mill Road															
Emergency stop															
Hill start															
Parking															
Reversing															
Signaling															

Record in this grid all the information obtained from the clues, by using a cross to indicate a definite "no" and a check to show a definite "yes." Transfer these to all sections of the grid thus eliminating all but one possibility, which must be the correct one.

279 · SPOT THE DIFFERENCES

Can you spot eight differences
between these two pictures of
carol singers?

Answer on page 497

280 · FILLING IN

Each of the nine empty boxes contains a different digit from 1 to 9. Can you fill in the empty boxes?

	+		÷		=	1
X		X		X		
	÷		−		=	2
÷		−		−		
	+		−		=	2

=		=		=
8		3		1

Answer on page 497

281 · FUNNY FAKES

The proud owners of the famous artist's paintings (top) are showing off their new acquisitions (bottom). Unfortunately, however, five of these are not really the artist's original work but are clever fakes. Which are the fakes and how can you identify them?

Answer on page 497

282 · A KNOTTY PROBLEM

Can you decide which one of these pieces of rope will be tied into a knot when both ends are pulled?

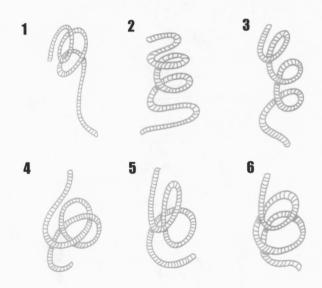

1

2

3

4

5

6

Answer on page 497

283 · COG-ITATE

Can you see which three weights will rise and which two will fall when the man pulls the rope?

Answer on page 497

284 · DAILY DOZEN

Here's a gentle mental exercise. Each of the twelve squares contains a different one of the numbers 1 to 12. From the clues given below, can you place them correctly?

Numbers: 1; 2; 3; 4; 5; 6; 7; 8; 9; 10; 11; 12

1 The 12 is in square B2; the numbers immediately to its left and diagonally below it to the left are both factors of it, one being an odd number.

2 The 6 is adjacent to the 10 in the same row, and is to be found in the same vertical column as the 8.

3 The numbers in squares A1 and C3 add up to the one in square C4.

4 The 7 is immediately below the 4, and immediately to the right of the 5.

	1	2	3	4
A				
B				
C				

5 Neither the 2 nor the 1 is in column 1, though the 2 is in a column farther left than the one containing the 11.

Note: The numbers that are proper factors of 12 are 1, 2, 3, 4, and 6.

Starting tip: First place the numbers referred to in clue 1.

Answer on page 497

Each picture is lacking in one detail that is present in the other seven. What are those details?

Answer on page 497

286 · A BOX IN THE SHED

When Joe needed something for a job around the house, he would say, "They're in a box in the shed." The four boxes shown in the diagram standing next to each other on a shelf, all of different colors, contain a different number of useful items. From the clues given below, can you work out the full details?

1. The 43 nails of assorted sizes are not in the brown box.
2. There are 58 items in the blue box.
3. The screws are in the green box, one of whose immediate neighbors on the shelf contains the washers, and the other the largest number of items.
4. The carpet tacks are in box C.

Box colors: blue; brown; green; red
Number: 39; 43; 58; 65
Items: carpet tacks; nails; screws; washers

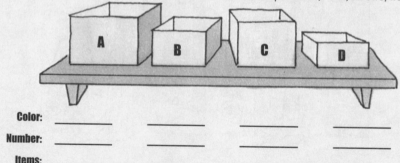

Color: _____ _____ _____ _____
Number: _____ _____ _____ _____
Items: _____ _____ _____ _____

Answer on page 497   Starting tip: First work out the color of the box containing the nails.

Look at the three clocks, then work out what the last clock should say to continue the sequence.

Answer on page 498

A standard set of dominoes has been laid out, using numbers instead of dots for clarity. Using a sharp pencil and a keen brain, can you draw in the lines to show where each domino has been placed? You may find the check grid useful—crossing off each domino as you find it.

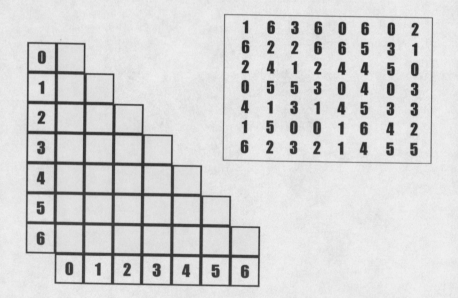

1	6	3	6	0	6	0	2
6	2	2	6	6	5	3	1
2	4	1	2	4	4	5	0
0	5	5	3	0	4	0	3
4	1	3	1	4	5	3	3
1	5	0	0	1	6	4	2
6	2	3	2	1	4	5	5

Answer on page 498

Study these objects carefully while someone times you for a minute, then close the book and see if you can remember them all.

This fireman isn't sure which hose is attached to the tap, and he needs to act fast! Can you help him out?

Answer on page 498

291 · IN THE ABSTRACT

George has bought one of the four abstract paintings on the right, but he can't remember which one it is or which way up it should go. Can you help him?

Answer on page 498

292 · SILHOUETTE

Shade in every fragment containing a dot—and what have you got?

Answer on page 498

293 · PILE UP

These piles of blocks aren't the random results of a child playing but clues to a final, at present blank, pile on the right. Like the rest, that one has six blocks each with a different one of the six letters. The numbers below the heaps tell you two things:

(a) The number of adjacent pairs of blocks in that column which also appear adjacent in the final pile.

(b) The number of adjacent pairs of blocks that make a correct pair but the wrong way up.

So:

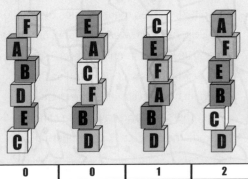

would score one in the "Correct" row if the final heap had an A directly above a C and one in the "Reversed" row if the final heap had a C on top of an A. From all this, can you create the final pile before it topples?

Correct	0	0	1	2		5
Reversed	0	1	0	1		0

Answer on page 498

Here's a tricky brainteaser for you. See how quickly you can work out how many candies each child has.

Some children are helping themselves to candies from a jar. David takes seven more candies than Sally, while Sally has six fewer than Tony, but twice as many as Katie. Simon has three more than Katie, who has twice as many as Philip. If Philip has two candies, how many did the others get, and how many candies do the children have altogether?

Answer on page 498

295 · ABC

Each line, across and down, should contain each of the letters A, B, and C, and two empty squares. The letter outside the grid shows the first or second letter in the direction of the arrow. Can you fill in the grid?

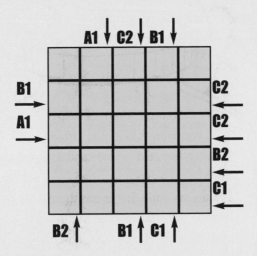

Can you spot eight differences between the two pictures?

Answer on page 498

297 · WOODWORK

Eight snapshots have been taken of the large scene. However, only four of them were taken at exactly the same time. Which four are they?

Answer on page 498

298 · DOT-TO-DOT

Something tells us this builder was reading his plans upside-down! Follow the dots to complete the scene.

Answer on page 498

299 · DOMINO SEARCH

A standard set of dominoes has been laid out, using numbers instead of dots for clarity. Using a sharp pencil and a keen brain, can you draw in the lines to show where each domino has been placed? You may find the check grid useful—crossing off each domino as you find it.

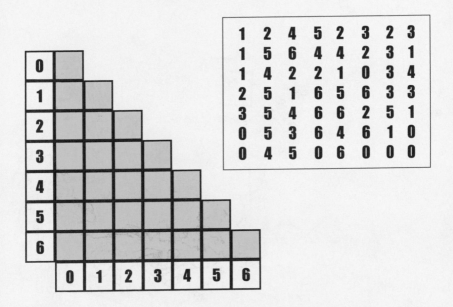

1	2	4	5	2	3	2	3
1	5	6	4	4	2	3	1
1	4	2	2	1	0	3	4
2	5	1	6	5	6	3	3
3	5	4	6	6	2	5	1
0	5	3	6	4	6	1	0
0	4	5	0	6	0	0	0

Answer on page 499

300 · BRAIN STRAINER

Every number on an upper story of the pyramid is the sum of the two numbers below it.
In this example the (?) must be a four, because 4+5 = 9: (9)
Begin at the base of the pyramid and climb to the top. (?)(5)

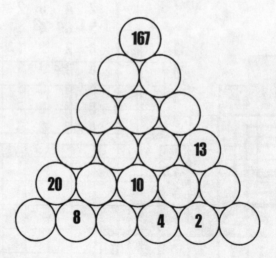

Answer on page 499

301 · LOGI-PATH

Use your deductive reasoning to form a pathway from START to FINISH moving either horizontally or vertically (but not diagonally). The number at the beginning of every row or column indicates exactly how many boxes in that row or column your pathway must pass through. The small diagram is given as an example of how it works.

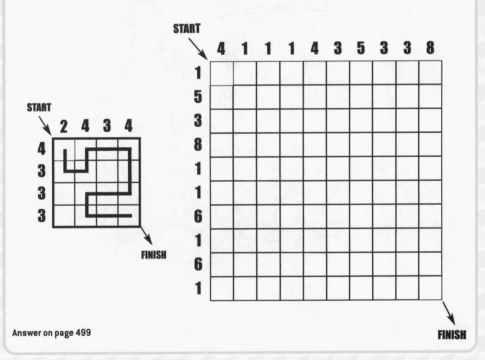

302 · CHANGE GEAR

While putting the final touches to his work, the artist notices that there are five discrepancies between his picture and the model. What are they?

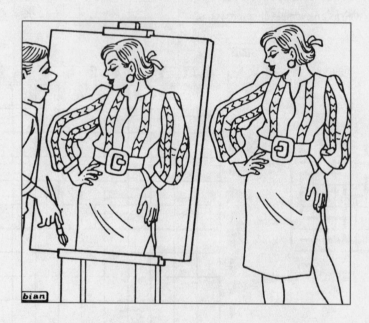

Answer on page 499

303 · NUMBER JIG

Fit the numbers into the grid as quickly as possible. One has been done for you.

3 figures	7718	450103
125	8154	485123
299	9501	510179
361		599126
420	**5 figures**	605544
584	19265	611683
713	28356	824916
~~882~~	34052	931152
	42166	
4 figures	61519	**7 figures**
1833		1385002
2985	**6 figures**	2439430
3772	102265	3226564
4421	176308	4748038
4506	236525	5360301
5055	251601	7243087
6909	309910	8011366

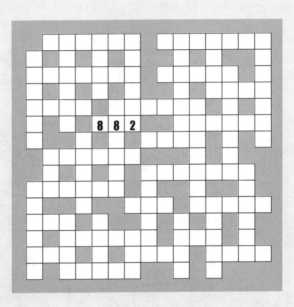

Answer on page 499

304 · SHORE THING

Two of these pictures are exactly the same, while each of the other two differs in one small detail from the rest. Can you spot the matching pictures and the differences?

Answer on page 499

305 · NUMBER SQUARES

Can you figure out the numbers that will fit into the empty squares and make each equation (across and down) correct?

Answer on page 499

306 · LOGI-5

Each line, across and down, is to have each of the letters A, B, C, D, and E, appearing once each. Also, every shape—shown by the thick lines—must have each of the letters in it. Can you fill in the grid?

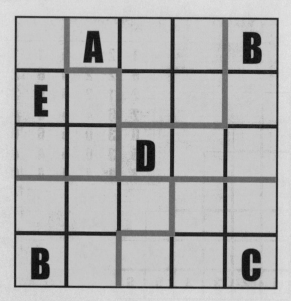

Answer on page 499

A standard set of dominoes has been laid out, using numbers instead of dots for clarity. Using a sharp pencil and a keen brain, can you draw in the lines to show where each domino has been placed? You may find the check grid useful—crossing off each domino as you find it.

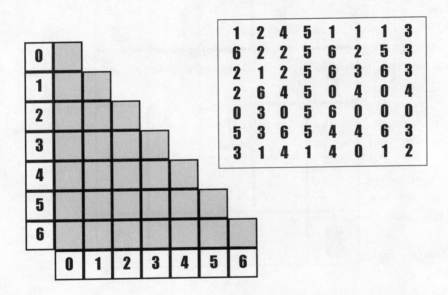

Answer on page 499

308 · TELL THE UNTRUTH

The four girls depicted in the diagram are all, we're afraid, inveterate little liars. From the clues given below, bearing in mind that every statement they make is untrue, can you correctly name the girl in each position, work out her true age, and describe the pet she owns?

Clues

1 Jenny says, "Hello, I'm nine, and I'm sitting in position 4."
2 Josie says, "Hi, I'm sitting next to my friend whose pet is a cat."
3 Jemima says, "Hello, I'm sitting next to Julie, whose pet is a tortoise, and my friend who owns the cat is nine."
4 Julie says, "Hi, my pet is the canary, and I'm eight years old. I'm in position 2 in the line."
5 To help you out, we'll tell you that the girl aged ten is in position 3, Josie's pet is a puppy, and the girl numbered 4 in the diagram has a canary.

Names: Jemima; Jenny; Josie; Julie
Ages: 8; 9; 10; 11
Pets: canary; cat; puppy; tortoise

Starting tip: Begin by identifying Julie's pet.

Answer on page 500

Name: _____ _____ _____ _____

Age: _____ _____ _____ _____

Pet: _____ _____ _____ _____

309 · TOY TRAILS

Ronnie has mixed up his remote control toys. Follow the lines to see which wire leads to which toy.

Answer on page 500

Can you see which two tangles will knot and which two will not?

Answer on page 500

311 · ON COURSE

Each of the lettered men must make their way along the paths to their respective destinations. Can you work out all four routes, bearing in mind that they can't use the same path and the paths must not cross?

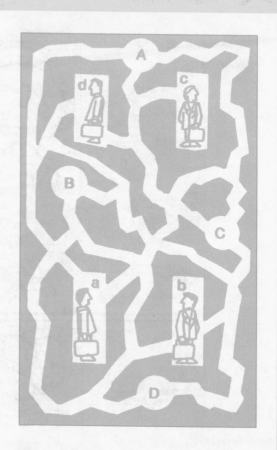

Answer on page 500

312 · RACE WINNERS

The large picture shows the start of a race and the small picture shows the eventual finishers.
Can you identify them?

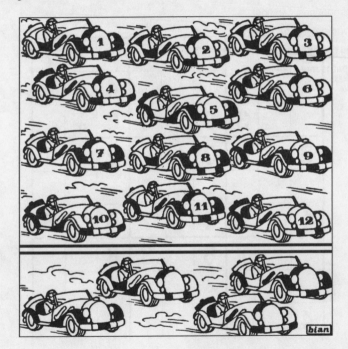

Answer on page 500

313 · SUDOKU

Place a number from 1 to 9 in each empty square so that each row, each column, and each 3x3 block contains all the numbers from 1 to 9.

9								7
		8				4		
		3	8		1	6		
8		4	3		6	2		1
1		5	4		7	9		8
		7	6		3	8		
		6				1		
4								5

Answer on page 500

314 · SILHOUETTE

Shade in every fragment containing a dot—and what have you got?

Answer on page 500

315 · LOGI-PATH

Use your deductive reasoning to form a pathway from START to FINISH moving either horizontally or vertically (but not diagonally). The number at the beginning of every row or column indicates exactly how many boxes in that row or column your pathway must pass through. The small diagram is given as an example of how it works.

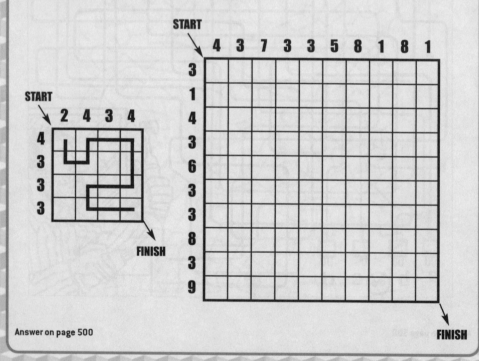

Answer on page 500

348

Which of the four plugs is connected to the toothbrush?

a b c d

Answer on page 500

Find your way across the clock faces. Watch out for the clock hands blocking the way.

Answer on page 500

318 · ABC

Each line, across and down, should contain each of the letters A, B, and C, and two empty squares. The letter outside the grid shows the first or second letter in the direction of the arrow. Can you fill in the grid?

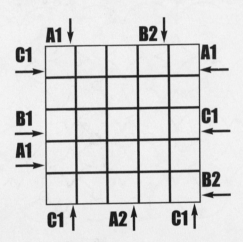

Answer on page 501

319 · TAIL TRAILS

These three have got their kites in a tangle! Follow the lines to match them back up.

Answer on page 501

320 · ABC

Each line, across and down, should contain each of the letters A, B, C, and D, and two empty squares. The letter outside the grid shows the first or second letter in the direction of the arrow. Can you fill in the grid?

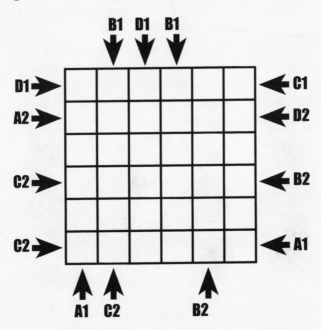

Answer on page 501

321 · PILE UP

These piles of blocks aren't the random results of a child playing but clues to a final, at present blank, pile on the right. Like the rest, that one has six blocks each with a different one of the six letters. The numbers below the heaps tell you two things:

(a) The number of adjacent pairs of blocks in that column which also appear adjacent in the final pile.

(b) The number of adjacent pairs of blocks that make a correct pair but the wrong way up.

So: would score one in the "Correct" row if the final heap had an A directly above a C and one in the "Reversed" row if the final heap had a C on top of an A. From all this, can you create the final pile before it topples?

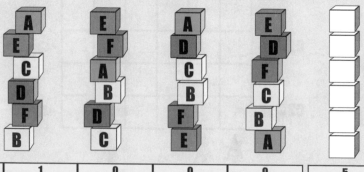

| Correct | 1 | 0 | 0 | 0 | 5 |
| Reversed | 0 | 0 | 2 | 2 | 0 |

Answer on page 501

322 · IN THE DEEP

Daisy the diver has lost her ring, and she can't seem to find it in the ocean. Can you find the ring, and then work your way through the maze from Daisy to it?

Answer on page 501

Which of the four numbered cubes is identical to the one held by the boy?

bian

Answer on page 501

Daisy and Joe are starring in the school play as the horse. But Daisy is late and Joe has lost all seven pieces of the costume! Help them out by finding the quickest route to the theater, picking up the costume on the way.

Answer on page 501

325 · SYMBOLISM

Each of the four symbols represents a certain number in all the rows across—and the across totals refer to the sum of the symbols shown on that row using these numbers. (Two different symbols can represent the same numbers.) Each symbol also refers to a number (it may or may not be the same number!) when used in the sums downward, with totals at the bottom of the grid—the symbols in each column add up to the totals at the bottom, and each symbol is the same number for all the downward sums.

Can you work out the value of the symbols shown, both horizontally and vertically?

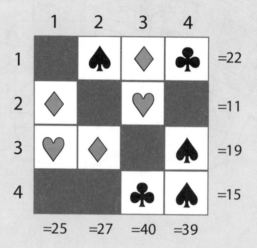

Answer on page 501

326 · BATTLESHIPS

Do you remember the old game of battleships? This puzzle is based on that idea. Your task is to find the vessels in the diagram. Some parts of boats or sea squares have already been filled in, and a number next to a row or column refers to the number of occupied squares in that row or column. The boats may be positioned horizontally or vertically, but no two boats or parts of boats are in adjacent squares—horizontally, vertically, or diagonally.

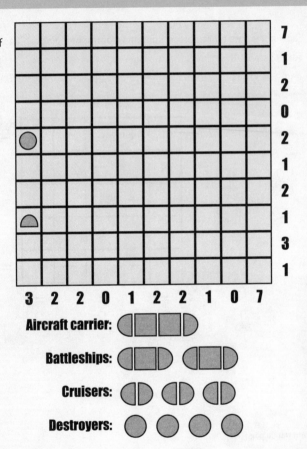

Aircraft carrier:

Battleships:

Cruisers:

Destroyers:

Answer on page 501

359

327 · FILLING IN

Each of the nine empty boxes contains a different digit from 1 to 9. Can you fill in the empty boxes?

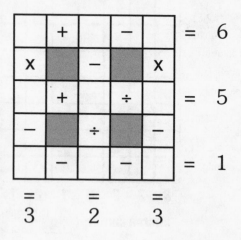

Answer on page 501

328 · BLACKOUT

Can you see which one of the letters is shown in negative form in the top left-hand corner?

Answer on page 501

Wilfred Worm wants to hurry home without disturbing that hungry-looking bird! Can you help him?

Home Sweet Home

Answer on page 501

Which two flowers are
exactly the same?

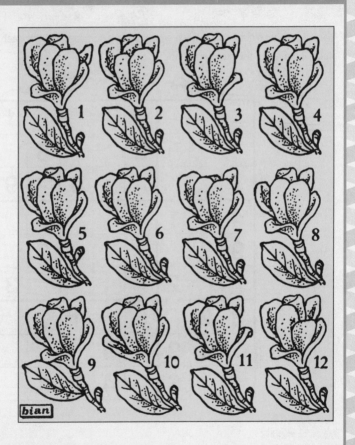

Answer on page 502

331 · SUDOKU

Place a number from 1 to 9 in each empty square so that each row, each column, and each 3x3 block contains all the numbers from 1 to 9.

							1	
			2			8		3
7				1	8		9	
4		1				5		
9	5					2		
		2					3	
8	9		6		1			
	4	3		9				
		6		4	7	3		

Answer on page 502

332 · THREE BY FOUR

Only three of the figures appear in all four rectangles—which ones are they?

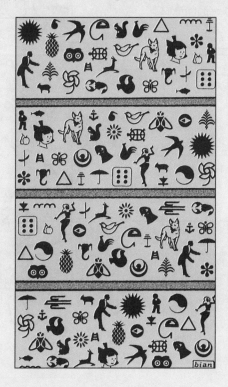

Answer on page 502

333 · COG-ITATE

When the engineer turns the handle, will the final cog move to touch pyramid 1 or pyramid 2?

Answer on page 502

334 · LOGI-5

Each line, across and down, is to have each of the letters A, B, C, D, and E, appearing once each. Also, every shape—shown by the thick lines—must have each of the letters in it. Can you fill in the grid?

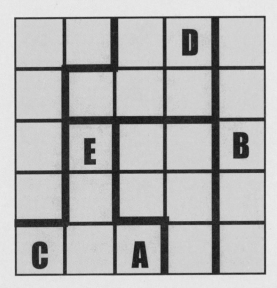

Answer on page 502

335 · SWINE LINES

Draw three straight lines from edge to edge to divide the box into five parts, each containing two pigs.

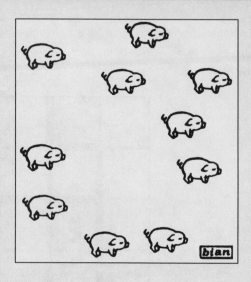

Answer on page 502

336 · BREAD WINNER

Two of these pictures are identical, while the other two differ slightly from the rest. Which are the "twins" and what are the differences?

Answer on page 502

337 · SILHOUETTE

Shade all the shapes that contain a dot to reveal a hidden picture.

Answer on page 502

Place a number from 1 to 9 in each empty square so that each row, each column, and each 3x3 block contains all the numbers from 1 to 9.

		4	9		6	8		
	8		4		1		5	
2		6	5		7	3		4
7	5	1				2	8	9
8	4	3				5	6	1
1		5	8		2	4		7
	7		3		4		2	
		2	7		5	6		

Answer on page 502

339 · ABC

Each line, across and down, should contain each of the letters A, B, and C, and two empty squares. The letter outside the grid shows the first or second letter in the direction of the arrow. Can you fill in the grid?

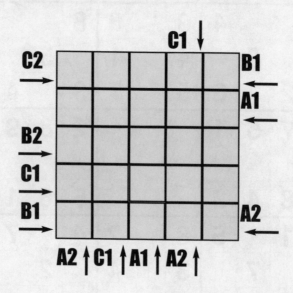

340 · SILHOUETTE

Shade all the shapes that contain a dot to reveal a picture.

Answer on page 502

These piles of blocks aren't the random results of a child playing but clues to a final, at present blank, pile on the right. Like the rest, that one has six blocks each with a different one of the six letters. The numbers below the heaps tell you two things:

(a) The number of adjacent pairs of blocks in that column which also appear adjacent in the final pile.

(b) The number of adjacent pairs of blocks that make a correct pair but the wrong way up.

So: would score one in the "Correct" row if the final heap had an A directly above a C and one in the "Reversed" row if the final heap had a C on top of an A. From all this, can you create the final pile before it topples?

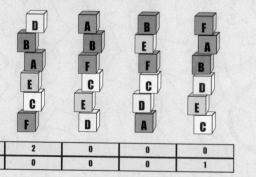

Correct	2	0	0	0		5
Reversed	0	0	0	1		0

Answer on page 503

342 · ACES HIGH

The four bridge players sitting around the table each had the ace of a different suit in his or her hand on the deal in question. From the clues given below, can you fully identify the player in each of the four seats, and work out which Ace each holds? Note: North and South play as partners against East and West.

Starting tip: Begin by working out which ace Richard held.

1 Richard's ace was the same color as the one held by Ruff, who was in the North seat.

2 Martina's partner was holding the ace of hearts.

3 The woman sitting West, whose surname is not Tenace, had the ace of spades.

4 Paul Hand was partnering Esther.

5 The ace of clubs was not held by the player sitting South.

First names: Esther; Martina; Paul; Richard

Surnames: Hand; Ruff; Tenace; Trick

Aces: Clubs; Diamonds; Hearts; Spades

First name: _____

Surname: _____

Ace: _____

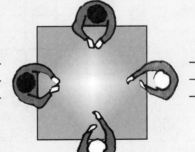

_____
_____
_____

_____
_____
_____

_____
_____
_____

Answer on page 503

343 · ABC

Each line, across and down, should contain each of the letters A, B, and C, and two empty squares. The letter outside the grid shows the first or second letter in the direction of the arrow. Can you fill in the grid?

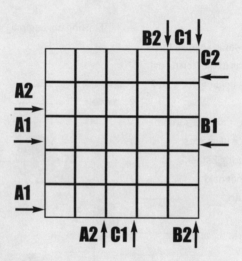

Answer on page 503

344 · TRILINES

Which three lines drawn from edge to edge divide the rectangle into five parts, each containing two ducklings?

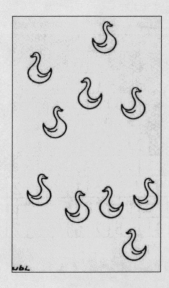

Answer on page 503

345 · SUMMIT

Go from the top of this pyramid (1) to its base, adding one block's value at each level to get a total of 55. You can only move from a block to one of its two lower neighbors.

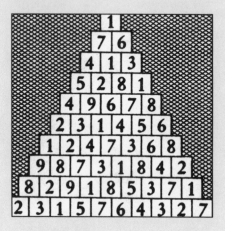

Answer on page 503

346 · CARTWHEELS

Which two numbered fragments complete wheel A, and which two complete wheel B?

Answer on page 503

347 · FRONT AND CENTER

The four central seats in each of the first three rows at the theater were all occupied at a recent performance. From the clues given below, can you place each of the listed people in their correct seats?

Clues

1 Peter was sitting directly behind Angela, and somewhere diagonally in front of Henry.

2 Nina had the ticket for seat 12 in row B.

3 The four seats featured in each row are occupied by two males and two females.

4 Maxine is two places to the right of Robert in the same row.

5 Judy, who is immediately behind Charles, has her husband Vincent as her right-hand neighbor.

6 One of the men in the audience is sitting in seat 13 of row A.

7 Tony, Janet, and Lydia all have seats in different rows, the latter having a male neighbor to her left.

Names: Angela; Charles; Henry; Janet; Judy; Lydia; Maxine; Nina; Peter; Robert; Tony; Vincent.

Answer on page 503

Starting tip: Begin by naming the man in seat 13 of row A.

Name: _____ _____ _____ _____

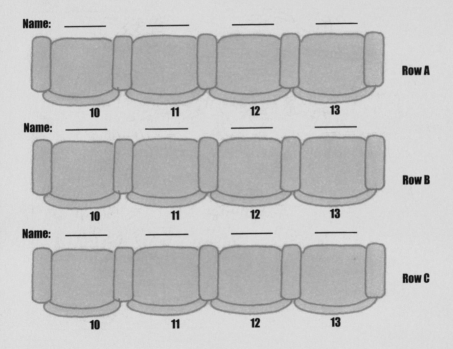

Row A

10   11   12   13

Name: _____ _____ _____ _____

Row B

10   11   12   13

Name: _____ _____ _____ _____

Row C

10   11   12   13

Which of the four numbered ends is the end of the clothesline?

Answer on page 504

349 · KNOT OR NOT

Which tangles will knot, and which will not, when their ends are pulled?

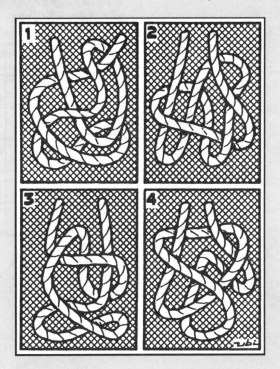

Answer on page 504

350 · ABC

Each line, across and down, should contain each of the letters A, B, C, and D, and two empty squares. The letter outside the grid shows the first or second letter in the direction of the arrow. Can you fill in the grid?

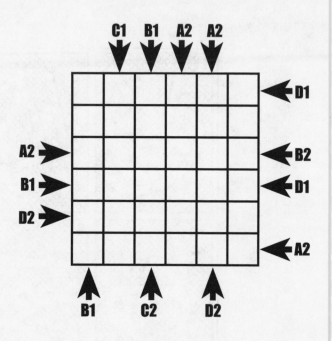

Answer on page 504

351 · TRAIL SAFE

Guide the little boy home from the candy shop by the shortest route. Make sure he doesn't bump into the bully!

Answer on page 504

From the information given on the right can you match each man to his wife?

Answer on page 504

A standard set of dominoes has been laid out, using numbers instead of dots for clarity. Using a sharp pencil and a keen brain, can you draw in the lines to show where each domino has been placed? You may find the check grid useful—crossing off each domino as you find it.

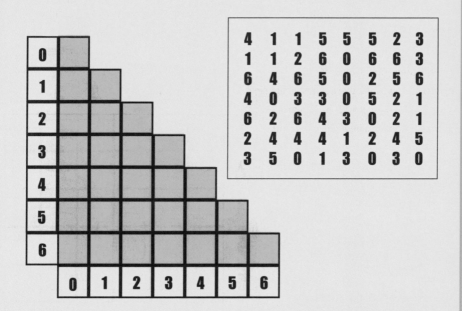

4	1	1	5	5	5	2	3
1	1	2	6	0	6	6	3
6	4	6	5	0	2	5	6
4	0	3	3	0	5	2	1
6	2	6	4	3	0	2	1
2	4	4	4	1	2	4	5
3	5	0	1	3	0	3	0

Answer on page 504

354 · FIGURE IT OUT

Each digit from 1 to 9 appears four times in the square, no similar digits being diagonally adjacent. Where the same digit appears more than once in any row or column, this is stated. Can you complete the square?

Row

1 Two 4s and two 9s; total 34

2 One even, two odd, two even, one odd digit from left to right; lowest is 2; total 37

3 Two 1s separated by an 8; two 5s but no 4s

4 Two adjacent 6s with an odd digit and two 8s

5 Two 3s separated by a 6; highest is a 7; total 22

6 Two adjacent 7s; total 24

Column

1 Two 8s separated by an odd digit; total 29

2 Two adjacent 9s; the other digits also total 18

3 Two adjacent 2s; total 27

4 Two 9s separated by two digits; total 31

5 Two 6s separated by two digits, all bracketed by two odd digits

6 Total 22

Answer on page 504

	1	**2**	**3**	**4**	**5**	**6**
1						
2						
3						
4						
5						
6						

355 · LOGI-5

Each line, across and down, is to have each of the letters A, B, C, D, and E, appearing once each. Also, every shape—shown by the thick lines—must have each of the letters in it. Can you fill in the grid?

Answer on page 504

356 · ABC

Each line, across and down, should contain each of the letters A, B, and C, and two empty squares. The letter outside the grid shows the first or second letter in the direction of the arrow. Can you fill in the grid?

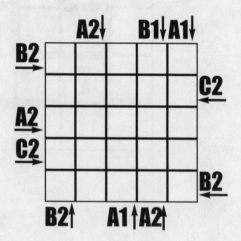

Answer on page 504

357 · NUMBER JIG

Fit the numbers into the grid as quickly as possible. One has been done for you.

3 figures	5018	**6 figures**
237	5106	138924
431	6362	183134
~~463~~	7290	237810
598	7910	265805
612	9306	327460
706		382412
813	**5 figures**	427894
934	11188	439013
	30128	509307
4 figures	48298	552609
1243	50021	635081
1390	73606	790296
2366	81834	808334
2395	82610	812847
3408		933321
4014		972801

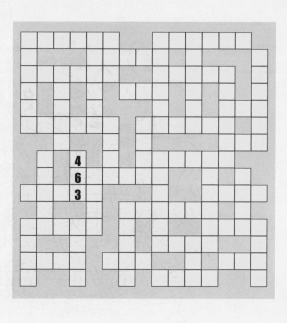

Answer on page 504

Follow the tangled trail to find out which pom-pom belongs to each of our poodle pals.

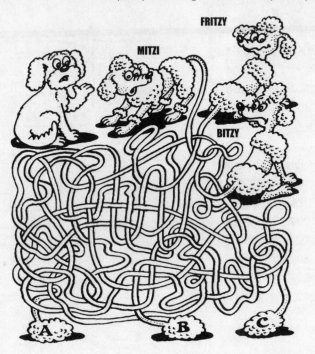

Answer on page 505

359 · IN A FLAP

Polly Parrot is very angry because she can't reach the big bag of seed that she wants for her dinner. Can you work out which path she should take to reach it?

Answer on page 505

360 · ABC

Each line, across and down, should contain each of the letters A, B, C, and D, and two empty squares. The letter outside the grid shows the first or second letter in the direction of the arrow. Can you fill in the grid?

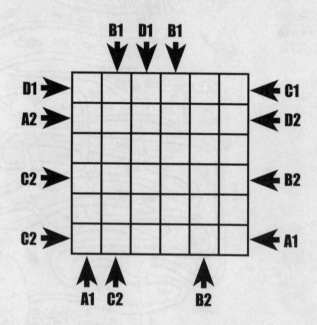

Answer on page 505

361 · MINIMAZE

Each obstacle along the maze's path carries a penalty (as shown in the key in the middle). Find your way from A to B incurring no more penalties than we did—36 in all.

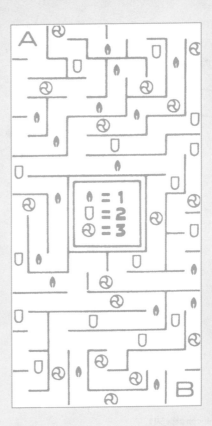

Answer on page 505

362 · COG-ITATE

If the engineer turns the handle in a clockwise direction, which one of the two numbered contacts will be touched?

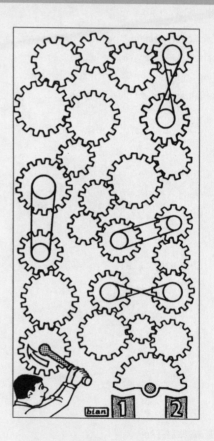

Answer on page 505

Answer on page 505

Shade in the shapes that contain a dot
to find out what's in the magic mirror!

Answer on page 505

365 · SUDOKU

Place a number from 1 to 9 in each empty square so that each row, each column, and each 3x3 block contains all the numbers from 1 to 9.

	3		2		1		6	
8		4				1		3
	1		9	3	4		2	
3		7	5		9	8		6
		6				3		
2		1	8		3	9		4
	7		1	4	6		3	
4		3				5		1
	9		3		8		4	

Answer on page 505

366 · LOGI-5

Each line, across and down, is to have each of the letters A, B, C, D, and E, appearing once each. Also, every shape—shown by the thick lines—must have each of the letters in it. Can you fill in the grid?

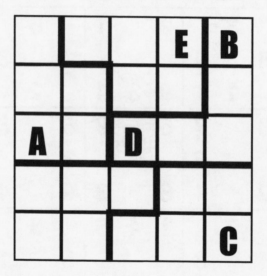

Answer on page 505

367 · SILHOUETTE

Shade in every fragment containing a dot—and what have you got?

Answer on page 505

Each line, across and down, should contain each of the letters A, B, and C, and two empty squares. The letter outside the grid shows the first or second letter in the direction of the arrow. Can you fill in the grid?

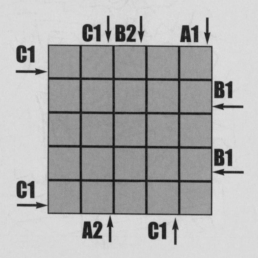

369 · PEEL ME A GRAPE

Four of the serving girls have mirror images. Which are the four pairs, and which is the odd girl out?

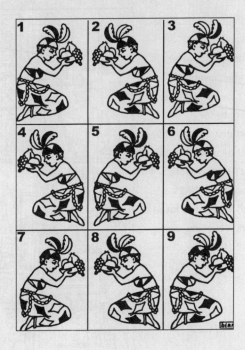

Answer on page 505

370 · FIND THE FAKES

The proud owners of the famous artist's paintings (shown on top) are showing off their new acquisitions (shown below). Unfortunately, however, five of these are not the artist's original work, but are clever fakes. Which are the five fakes and how can you identify them?

Answer on page 506

371 · SUDOKU

Place a number from 1 to 9 in each empty square so that each row, each column, and each 3x3 block contains all the numbers from 1 to 9.

	8		1		7		4	
6		7				3		5
	2		8	5	6		1	
2		8		6		5		3
		6	5		3	8		
1		3		9		4		6
	6		7	1	2		3	
7		2				1		4
	3		6		9		5	

Answer on page 506

Which of the seven impressions was made by the stamp?

Answer on page 506

373 · BATTLESHIPS

Do you remember the old game of battleships? This puzzle is based on that idea. Your task is to find the vessels in the diagram. Some parts of boats or sea squares have already been filled in, and a number next to a row or column refers to the number of occupied squares in that row or column. The boats may be positioned horizontally or vertically, but no two boats or parts of boats are in adjacent squares—horizontally, vertically, or diagonally.

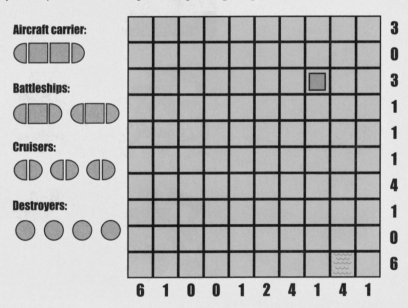

Aircraft carrier:

Battleships:

Cruisers:

Destroyers:

3
0
3
1
1
1
4
1
0
6

6 1 0 0 1 2 4 1 4 1

Answer on page 506

374 · BLACKOUT

Can you see which one of the letters is shown in negative form in the top left-hand corner?

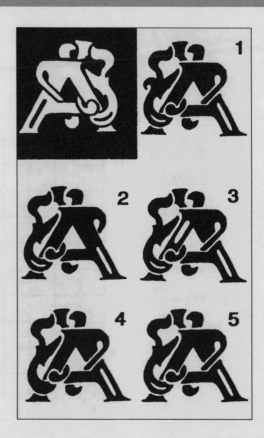

Answer on page 506

Follow the dots from 1 to 49 to reveal the hidden picture.

Answer on page 506

Which one of the six numbered drawers will match up with those already in place?

Answer on page 506

377 · LOGI-5

Each line, across and down, is to have each of the letters A, B, C, D, and E, appearing once each. Also, every shape—shown by the thick lines—must have each of the letters in it. Can you fill in the grid?

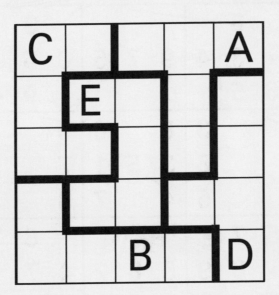

Answer on page 506

Place a number from 1 to 9 in each empty square so that each row, each column, and each 3x3 block contains all the numbers from 1 to 9.

	8						3	
	3	4	9	7	5	8	6	
6	5						9	4
		3	8		6	9		
		6	3	5	1	7		
		5	4		7	3		
5	7						8	3
	6	9	5	8	2	4	7	
	2						5	

Answer on page 506

Freddie the fisherman is in trouble. Can you lead the lifeguard to him, avoiding the perils of the sea along the way?

Answer on page 506

380 · LOGI-5

Each line, across and down, is to have each of the letters A, B, C, D, and E, appearing once each. Also, every shape—shown by the thick lines—must have each of the letters in it. Can you fill in the grid?

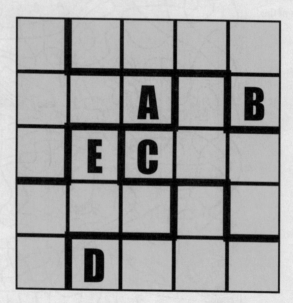

Answer on page 506

381 · ABC

Each line, across and down, should contain each of the letters A, B, and C, and two empty squares. The letter outside the grid shows the first or second letter in the direction of the arrow. Can you fill in the grid?

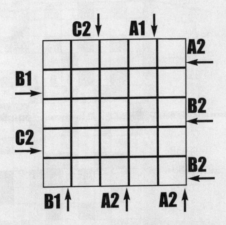

Answer on page 506

382 · NUMBER JIG

Fit the numbers into the grid as quickly as possible. One has been done for you.

3 figures
179
331
407 (crossed out)
523
658
669
918

4 figures
1646
2375
3498
4582
4981
5259
6144
7076

5 figures
18260
24887
42325
43148
85239

6 figures
119715
122552
193277
225463
280648
337594
445717

7704
8817
569857
646303
802208
851707
912661
978522

7 figures
1233067
1694459
2116689
3428729
7455454
8973135
9301231

Answer on page 507

383 · LOGI-5

Each line, across and down, is to have each of the letters A, B, C, D, and E, appearing once each. Also, every shape—shown by the thick lines—must have each of the letters in it. Can you fill in the grid?

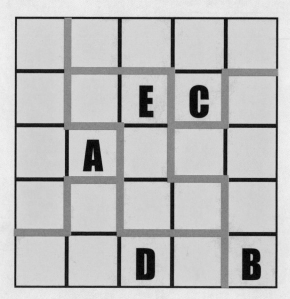

Answer on page 507

Acchooo! All these feathers are making us sneeze. How quickly can you put the pictures in order, from the smallest feather to the largest feather?

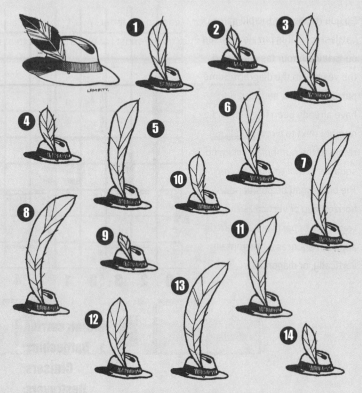

Answer on page 507

385 · BATTLESHIPS

Do you remember the old game of battleships? This puzzle is based on that idea. Your task is to find the vessels in the diagram. Some parts of boats or sea squares have already been filled in, and a number next to a row or column refers to the number of occupied squares in that row or column. The boats may be positioned horizontally or vertically, but no two boats or parts of boats are in adjacent squares—horizontally, vertically, or diagonally.

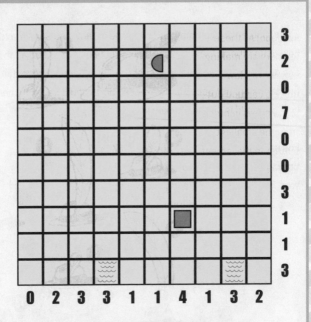

Row totals (top to bottom): 3, 2, 0, 7, 0, 0, 3, 1, 1, 3

Column totals (left to right): 0, 2, 3, 3, 1, 1, 4, 1, 3, 2

Aircraft carrier:

Battleships:

Cruisers:

Destroyers:

Answer on page 507

386 · TENTACKLE

Eight children are camping out, two to each tent, and some have given us a couple of clues as to how to find them. The trouble is their directions are as bad as their cooking and in each case only one direction is true while the other is an exact opposite, so that east should read west, etc. Directions are not necessarily exact so north could be north, northeast, or northwest. To help you, one child is already tucked into a sleeping bag.

Ros says: "I'm south of Sue and east of Xena."
Una says: "I'm north of Zoe and west of Ros."
Viv says: "I'm north of Wendy and west of Una."
Xena says: "I'm south of Trish and east of Sue."

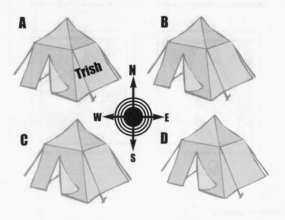

Answer on page 507

To the left are four abstract paintings. To the right Jim is trying to work out which one he's bought and which way up it's supposed to be. Can you help him?

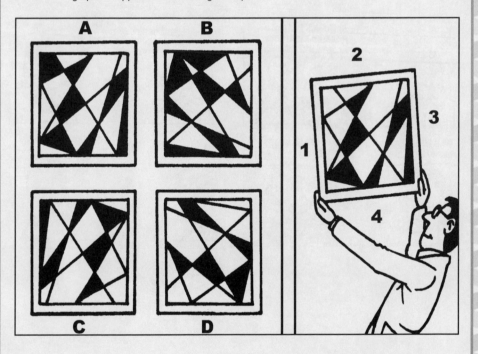

Answer on page 507

Using the information given, match each man to his wife.

Answer on page 507

389 · OFF FORM

Which one of the eight numbered pieces is the one that is missing from the broken bench?

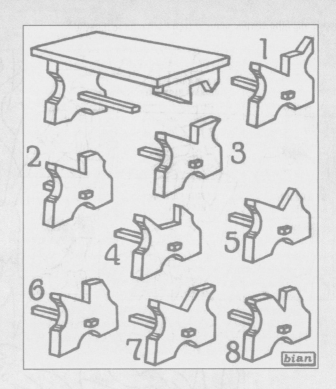

Answer on page 507

390 · SILHOUETTE

Shade all of the shapes containing a dot to reveal a picture.

Answer on page 507

391 · CUT UP

In what order must the five numbered pieces be arranged to form the complete strip shown at the top?

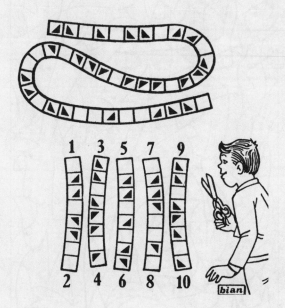

Answer on page 507

392 · FOURSOME

This man would like to buy four identical vases. Which design will he choose?

Answer on page 507

Can you match up the numbered keys with their respective locks?

Answer on page 507

Follow the dots from 1 to 42 to reveal the hidden picture.

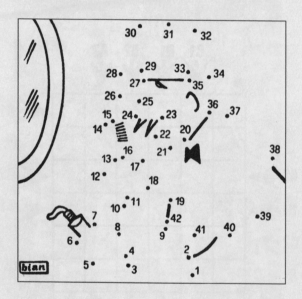

Answer on page 507

395 · ABC

Each line, across and down, should contain each of the letters A, B, C, and D, and two empty squares. The letter outside the grid shows the first or second letter in the direction of the arrow. Can you fill in the grid?

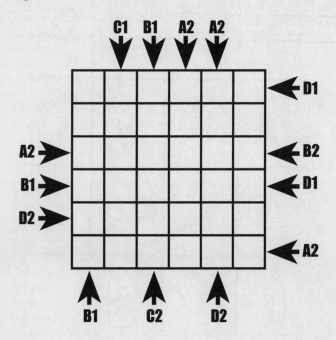

Answer on page 508

396 · SYMBOLIC

Can you work out which symbol should logically appear in the empty box and which way up it should be?

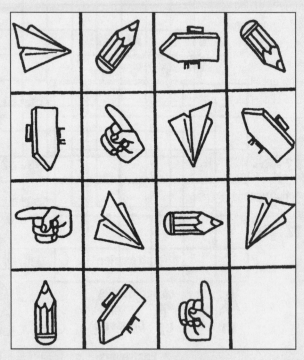

Answer on page 508

397 · BATTLESHIPS

Do you remember the old game of battleships? This puzzle is based on that idea. Your task is to find the vessels in the diagram. Some parts of boats or sea squares have already been filled in, and a number next to a row or column refers to the number of occupied squares in that row or column. The boats may be positioned horizontally or vertically, but no two boats or parts of boats are in adjacent squares—horizontally, vertically, or diagonally.

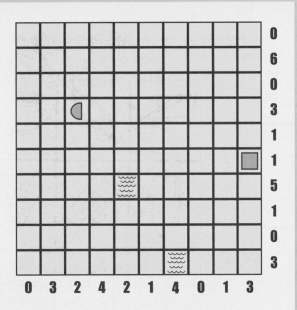

Aircraft carrier:

Battleships:

Cruisers:

Destroyers:

Answer on page 508

398 · IDENTICAL TWINS

Which of these two
pictures are
identical?

A B C D E F

Answer on page 508

399 · NUMBER JIG

Fit the numbers into the grid as quickly as possible. One has been done for you.

3 figures	4271	60774
183	9928	62055
186		63044
233	**5 figures**	63715
269	10264	68133
311	13956	70222
312	15828	70998
484	21190	71605
550	23104	73930
610	24526	81464
706	26866	81995
830	33009	88921
~~849~~	41084	
872	41544	**6 figures**
955	42083	142738
	43265	236007
4 figures	51300	420316
1002	51900	523481
3815	57134	913345

The grid contains the entry **8 4 9** already filled in.

Answer on page 508

400 · TWISTING TRAILS

Help Rockin' Ron find his way to the stage door so that the show can go on!

STAGE DOOR

CONCERT

TONIGHT

Answer on page 508

401 · LOGI-5

Each line, across and down, is to have each of the letters A, B, C, D, and E, appearing once each. Also, every shape—shown by the thick lines—must have each of the letters in it. Can you fill in the grid?

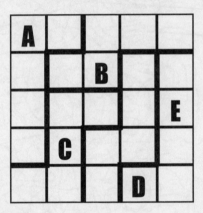

Answer on page 508

Follow the vines to see what
Sue's trying to find!

Answer on page 508

403 · ABC

Each line, across and down, should contain each of the letters A, B, and C, and two empty squares. The letter outside the grid shows the first or second letter in the direction of the arrow. Can you fill in the grid?

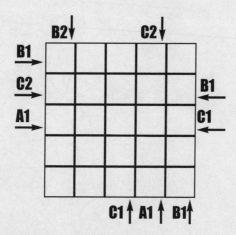

John, Joe, and Sue are having fun! Can you work out which prize each child is going to win?

Answer on page 508

There are two identical butterflies on this page. Which two are they?

Answer on page 508

406 · GUYS IN THE BLACK HATS

The four posters on the wall of the sheriff's office in the Wild West town of Redrock show the members of the notorious Black Hat Gang of train robbers. From the clues given below, can you fill in each outlaw's first name, nickname, and surname?

1 Herbert's picture is horizontally adjacent to that of "Butch" McColl.

2 Poster A shows Jacob, but Silvester Jaggard isn't depicted on poster C.

3 The poster with a picture of the man surnamed Wolf is horizontally adjacent to the one that shows the one nicknamed "Pony."

4 Churchman, who appears on poster D, isn't the outlaw nicknamed "Apache."

Starting tip: Work out the first name of the bad guy on poster C.

First names: Herbert; Jacob; Matthew; Silvester
Nicknames: Apache; Butch; Pony; Rio
Surnames: Churchman; Jaggard; McColl; Wolf

Answer on page 509

407 · LOGI-5

Each line, across and down, is to have each of the letters A, B, C, D, and E, appearing once each. Also, every shape—shown by the thick lines—must have each of the letters in it. Can you fill in the grid?

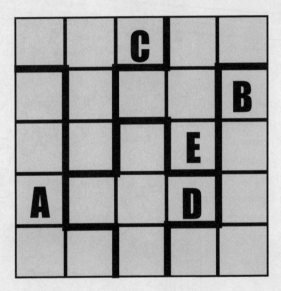

Answer on page 509

Alec has invented a teddy
bear—making machine.
Which two teddies are
identical?

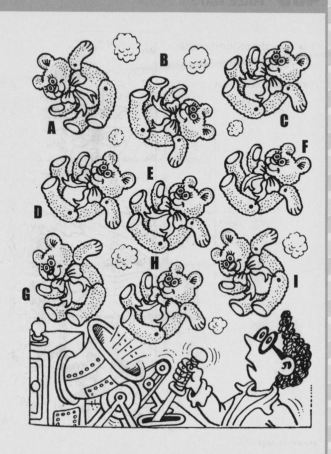

Answer on page 509

How does the photographer reach the rare rhinopotomus without crossing any lines?

Answer on page 509

Shade all the shapes that have a dot in, to find out what's going on here.

Answer on page 509

411 · PILE UP

These piles of blocks aren't the random results of a child playing but clues to a final, at present blank, pile on the right. Like the rest, that one has six blocks each with a different one of the six letters. The numbers below the heaps tell you two things:

(a) The number of adjacent pairs of blocks in that column which also appear adjacent in the final pile.

(b) The number of adjacent pairs of blocks that make a correct pair but the wrong way up.

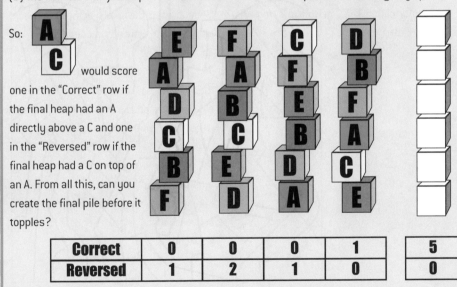

So: would score one in the "Correct" row if the final heap had an A directly above a C and one in the "Reversed" row if the final heap had a C on top of an A. From all this, can you create the final pile before it topples?

| Correct | 0 | 0 | 0 | 1 | | 5 |
| Reversed | 1 | 2 | 1 | 0 | | 0 |

Answer on page 509

Amy Witherspoon is a methodical soul who believes that routine equals efficiency. When she retired recently after working for 45 years in a department store, she organized her week so that she has one principal activity every morning, afternoon, and evening. From the following information, can you work out Amy's Monday-to-Friday timetable?

Clues

A Monday is the day for mopping the kitchen floor, but not for choir practice; Amy does her weekly shop on Tuesday.

B Wash day is immediately followed by ironing day, which is not on the same day as going to either the library or the art class, both of which activities occur on different days.

C Amy does her baking on the morning of her friend's visit, so that they can have fresh cakes for tea, and so that Amy can take some to her sister, whom she visits the next afternoon.

D The weekly whist game takes place the day after bingo and the day before Amy does her ironing; she likes to have her hair done on Friday, so that she looks her best for the weekend.

Answer on page 509

	Morning					Afternoon					Evening				
	Baking	Ironing	Mopping	Polishing	Washing	Friend	Hairdresser	Library	Shops	Sister	Art class	Bingo	Choir	Television	Whist
Monday															
Tuesday															
Wednesday															
Thursday															
Friday															
Art class															
Bingo															
Choir															
Television															
Whist															
Friend															
Hairdresser															
Library															
Shops															
Sister															

Record in this grid all the information obtained from the clues, by using a cross to indicate a definite "no" and a check to show a definite "yes." Transfer these to all sections of the grid thus eliminating all but one possibility, which must be the correct one.

Day	Morning	Afternoon	Evening

413 · SUDOKU

Place a number from 1 to 9 in each empty square so that each row, each column, and each 3x3 block contains all the numbers from 1 to 9.

		6		8		7		
		3	9	7	1	6		
8	5		4		6		1	9
	8	4				1	7	
6	2						9	8
	7	9				5	2	
1	3		8		4		5	7
		5	2	3	7	8		
		8		1		2		

Answer on page 509

414 · PILE UP

These piles of blocks aren't the random results of a child playing but clues to a final, at present blank, pile on the right. Like the rest, that one has six blocks each with a different one of the six letters. The numbers below the heaps tell you two things:

(a) The number of adjacent pairs of blocks in that column which also appear adjacent in the final pile.

(b) The number of adjacent pairs of blocks that make a correct pair but the wrong way up.

So:

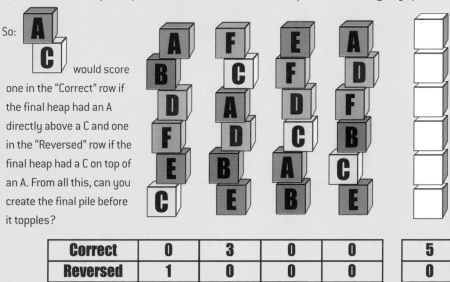

would score one in the "Correct" row if the final heap had an A directly above a C and one in the "Reversed" row if the final heap had a C on top of an A. From all this, can you create the final pile before it topples?

Correct	0	3	0	0		5
Reversed	1	0	0	0		0

Answer on page 509

415 · STARRY EYED

Louise is upset because the stars her teacher stuck in her math book have become unstuck. How many stars and how many tears can you find hidden in this picture?

Answer on page 509

Which four of the twelve urns are identical?

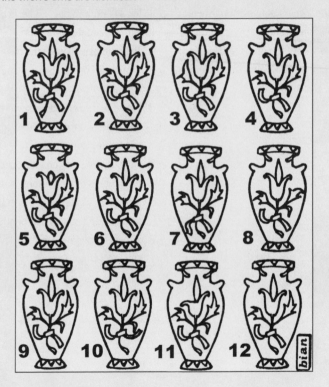

Answer on page 510

Canine psychiatrist Jack Russell has been consulted by the owners of five animals with behavioral problems. From the clues on the right, can you work out the name and breed of each person's pet, and say what its problem is?

Clues

1 Miss Flatman's dog, Eddie, is not the whippet with a morbid fear of cats.

2 The animal with what the owner describes as "antisocial habits" has a name beginning with a consonant.

3 Owing to the misplaced generosity of the customers at the bar run by his owner, Flash has become an alcoholic.

4 Ms. Scanlon's dog chases policemen, but ignores other persons in uniform.

5 Mrs. Carrick's pet, which isn't the boxer, is sociable and has no fear of other animals.

6 King is a Dalmatian, but Outlaw is not Mr. McCrae's corgi.

Answer on page 510

	Eddie	Flash	King	Outlaw	Tiffany	Boxer	Corgi	Dalmatian	Red Setter	Whippet	Alcoholic	Antisocial habits	Chases policemen	Eats flowers	Scared of cats
Mr. Baker															
Mrs. Carrick															
Miss Flatman															
Mr. McCrae															
Ms. Scanlon															
Alcoholic															
Antisocial habits															
Chases policemen															
Eats flowers															
Scared of cats															
Boxer															
Corgi															
Dalmatian															
Red Setter															
Whippet															

Record in this grid all the information obtained from the clues, by using a cross to indicate a definite "no" and a check to show a definite "yes." Transfer these to all sections of the grid thus eliminating all but one possibility, which must be the correct one.

Owner	Dog	Breed	Problem

Shade all the shapes containing
a dot to reveal the picture.

Answer on page 510

419 · BLACK AND WHITE

Put some black in this black and white movie by finding and shading the shapes at the bottom, in the screen.

Answer on page 510

The numbers alongside each row or column tell you how many blocks of black squares are in a line. For example: 2, 3, 5 tells you that from left to right (or top to bottom) there is a group of two black squares, then at least one white square, then a group of three black squares, then at least one white square, then a group of five black squares. Each block of black squares on the same line must have at least one white square between it and the next block of black squares.

Sometimes it is possible to tell which squares are going to be black without reference to other lines or columns. In the example below, we can deduce that any block of six black squares must incorporate the two central squares:

6 ▢▢▢▢▢■■▢▢▢▢

Can you complete this hanjie puzzle to reveal the hidden pattern or picture?

Answer on page 510

			1 1 3	3 3 1	3 4	3 1	3 1 1	3 4 3	3 1 1	3 2 1	3 1 1	4 1	3 3 1 5	2 1 2	2
	1	4	5	1	9	9	1	3	1	1	1	1	1	2	2
	3	4	1	9	9	8	8	1	8	9	9	9	1	4	3
7															
9															
9															
2 2															
1 2 2 1															
2 1 1 2															
1 1 1															
2 1 2 2															
1 2 2 1															
2 2 2 2															
3 1 3															
1 3 1 3 1															
1 9 1															
7 7															
6 6															
6 6															
6 6															
5 5															
4 4															
1 7 1															

421 · SUDOKU

Place a number from 1 to 9 in each empty square so that each row, each column, and each 3x3 block contains all the numbers from 1 to 9.

				9			7	
			4		7	2		6
7		9	3			4		8
9	2					3		5
6		5						
3	7					1		9
5		8	1			6		4
			6		2	9		1
				4			3	

Answer on page 510

422 · THE INVISIBLES

Many of the people in this circus scene are plainly visible. However, there are several more whose presence can only be inferred from various details in the picture. Can you expose the "missing persons?"

Answer on page 511

423 · ABC

Each line, across and down, should contain each of the letters A, B, and C, and two empty squares. The letter outside the grid shows the first or second letter in the direction of the arrow. Can you fill in the grid?

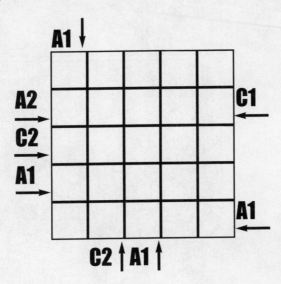

Answer on page 511

Despite their hidden faces, the criminals involved in the four scenes at the top were soon arrested by a smart detective who identified them from other details. Can you spot the clues?

Answer on page 511

425 · THAT LITTLE BIT OF DIFFERENCE

There are eight differences between the two cartoons. Can you spot them?

Answer on page 511

On each of the approach roads to our village stands a listed building that no longer serves its original purpose, but has been converted into a residence. From the clues given on the right, can you describe the purpose for which each of the buildings numbered 1 to 4 was first designed, say in which year it was built, and name its present owners?

Buildings: inn; railway station; tollhouse; windmill

Dates: 1761; 1772; 1825; 1854

Owners: Carter; Lewis; Morton; Vickers

Clues

1 The railway station is the most recent building, having been erected in 1854; it is on the road 90 degrees clockwise from the one on which the property where the Mortons live stands.

2 The building you pass as you enter the village from the north was built in 1825.

3 You go straight on at the crossroads to get from the building dating from 1772 to the old windmill; neither of these buildings now belongs to the Vickers family.

4 Building 3 is older than the one where the Carters live, but not as old as the one-time tollhouse.

5 The home of the Lewis family, which bears an even number on the plan, dates from the 18th century.

Answer on page 511

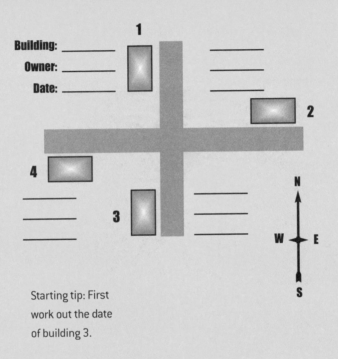

Building: _____

Owner: _____

Date: _____

Starting tip: First
work out the date
of building 3.

427 · CROSSED LINES

Which one of these four numbered toy ducks is being pulled by the boy?

bian

Answer on page 511

Can you see which one of the five boxes is the same as that being held by the magician? The two sides are visible in the identical box as well.

Answer on page 511

429 · HANJIE

The numbers alongside each row or column tell you how many blocks of black squares are in a line. For example: 2, 3, 5 tells you that from left to right (or top to bottom) there is a group of two black squares, then at least one white square, then a group of three black squares, then at least one white square, then a group of five black squares. Each block of black squares on the same line must have at least one white square between it and the next block of black squares.

Sometimes it is possible to tell which squares are going to be black without reference to other lines or columns. In the example below, we can deduce that any block of six black squares must incorporate the two central squares:

6 ⬜⬜⬜⬜⬛⬛⬜⬜⬜⬜

Can you complete this hanjie puzzle to reveal the hidden pattern or picture?

Answer on page 511

Column clues:

Column	Clues
1	2 14 5 9
2	17 2 3 8
3	14 4 3 7
4	12 8 3 6
5	11 10 3 5
6	11 3 2 2 3 4
7	11 2 4 1 2 3 3
8	10 3 2 1 2 3 2
9	10 4 2 3 1
10	10 7 2 3
11	9 7 2 3
12	9 3 2 2
13	9 2 2 1
14	9 2 2
15	9 1 2
16	9 1 2
17	9 1 3
18	9 1 1 2
19	8 1 2 2
20	7 1 2 1
21	7 1 3 1
22	6 1 1 1 1
23	6 1 3 4 1
24	5 2 1 2 1 1 1
25	5 6 1 1 2 2
26	4 1 2 11
27	4 2 1 2
28	3 2 1 6
29	2 2 1 7
30	2 2 3
31	1 6
32	6
33	6
34	6
35	5

Row clues:

Row	Clues
1	2 13
2	21
3	23
4	24
5	25
6	27
7	28
8	30
9	19 5
10	10 7
11	7 9 2
12	5 7 1
13	4 7 1
14	3 7 4 1
15	2 3 3 3 1 2
16	2 2 2 2 1 4 2
17	2 2 2 2 2
18	1 3 1 1 2
19	1 3 2 2
20	5 1 1
21	7 6
22	1 2 1 1
23	1 2 1 1
24	2 3 1 1
25	3 3 5
26	3 2 3
27	1 3 2 3 2
28	2 3 2 2 2
29	3 3 2 1 2
30	4 3 2 1 2 5
31	5 3 2 1 2 2 5
32	6 3 2 7 7
33	7 3 4 7
34	8 3 2 6
35	9 3 1 4

There was panic in the court of King Brian when five of the monarch's food-tasters fell ill on consecutive days. At first it was thought that someone was trying to poison the king, but it soon became clear that the cause of the problem was the new chef, whose cooking was so terrible that it was a hazard to human health. From the clues given on the right, can you work out the order in which the tasters became unwell, discover which food gave each of them food poisoning, and for which meal it was to be served?

Answer on page 511

Clues

1 Jasper was the taster who was affected immediately before the one who felt distinctly odd after eating some turkey.

2 Eric contracted food poisoning by sampling something intended for the king's lunch one day.

3 The fourth taster to fall ill suffered an unpleasant reaction to some poorly cooked goose.

4 Chicken was not responsible for laying low the second taster, Alan, who was not the man affected by food prepared for the king's light supper one evening.

5 Oswald, who was not the first taster to become unwell, got food poisoning from some beef, and the very next taster to fall victim to the chef's cooking was poisoned by food due to be served as part of the king's afternoon snack.

6 The last of the five tasters to fall ill did so as a result of eating food intended for a huge evening banquet.

	Alan	Eric	Jasper	Oswald	Percival	Beef	Chicken	Goose	Pork	Turkey	Afternoon snack	Evening banquet	Light supper	Lunch	Morning snack
First															
Second															
Third															
Fourth															
Fifth															
Afternoon snack															
Evening banquet															
Light supper															
Lunch															
Morning snack															
Beef															
Chicken															
Goose															
Pork															
Turkey															

Record in this grid all the information obtained from the clues, by using a cross to indicate a definite "no" and a check to show a definite "yes." Transfer these to all sections of the grid thus eliminating all but one possibility, which must be the correct one.

Order	Taster	Food	Meal

1

From the top: F, D, A, B, C, E.

2

7 – 38, 9 – 30, 18 – 47.

3

	B	C		A
		A	B	C
A	C			B
C		B	A	
B	A		C	

4

Number 4.

5

2	2	1	5	5	■	4	4	4	4	4
5	■	■	0	■	8	■	■	■	4
2	■	2	8	8	■	4	8	8	■	3
8	1	4	■	■	2	■	■	1	1	1
1	■	1	2	6	1	1	2	9	■	0
■	■	2	1	1	1	7	5	5	■	■
2	■	4	9	0	6	2	2	5	■	4
2	4	4	■	■	0	■	■	1	2	4
3	■	1	5	5	■	1	5	9	■	4
5	■	■	1	■	0	■	■	■	5
2	2	2	2	2	■	1	1	2	3	0

The combination is 2111755.

6

The middle one and the bottom one in the first column, and the top in the third column.

7

8

Picture 1 has an extra detail on the butt of the gun. Picture 2 has a sight added to the barrel of the gun. Picture 3 has an extra detail on the helmet. Picture 4 has an extra triangle above the belt.

9

Number 3, with side B at the top.

10

Pictures B and C are identical. Picture A has a circular rear view mirror.

Picture D has a couchlike front seat compared to the others which have two single front seats.

11

Squares 2a, 5d, and 10a.

12

The collector chose snail f.

13

14

Kites: A = 2; B = 4; C = 3; D = 1.

15

C			A	B
	B	C		A
A		B		C
	C	A	B	
B	A		C	

16

17

1B–4B, 2B–5D, 2D–9D, 7D–9A, 6A–5G, 3D–6D.

18

2	3	5	7	9	4	1	6	8
6	9	1	8	2	5	4	3	7
7	8	4	3	6	1	5	2	9
9	6	7	5	4	8	2	1	3
5	1	2	6	3	7	9	8	4
8	4	3	2	1	9	6	7	5
4	2	6	9	8	3	7	5	1
3	5	9	1	7	6	8	4	2
1	7	8	4	5	2	3	9	6

19

The professor bought book B.

20

Plug D.

21

22

1	0	3	4	5	1	2	4
6	5	0	0	0	2	3	4
3	1	6	1	2	4	4	6
6	1	5	5	0	3	3	2
6	4	0	4	5	6	3	5
5	3	2	1	3	1	0	5
6	0	1	6	2	2	2	4

23

```
2 9 9 1   5 1 2 7 9   8 3 4 1
1     3   7       0   3       7
2     2 1 5 4 3     1 9 0 6 6 8
4 0 5 7       2 1 2         0
      5 5 8 8   0       6 0 4 8
3 7 5       4 3 1 2 5       1 1
      8 1 0 6       7 8 9 1   7
7 1 5       6 5 4 3 2   5   5 3
      4 5 6 7 8     6 2 6 2 0 6
      4     1 4 0 7 4 7     9
      4     8     5     3 0 1 7
9 8 3 1 4       4 5 6 8 7 0 0
8       8 7 6 5 3   5     4 0 0
6       0       2   4     6 0 0
7 1 4 2     9 0 1 0 3     5 0 0 0
```

24

8	2	6	1
6	4	1	5
1	8	5	2
4	6	3	8

25

1E–2C, 3E–4A, 2B–7B, 4B–8B, 7F–9G, 3G–4C.

26

Squares D5, C1, F5, D2, and B1.

27

28

6, K, 9, A, 8, Q, 4, J, 2, 7, 10, 3, 5.

471

29

30

1 The piece at the lower right of the computer; 2 The hands of the clock; 3 The handle to the side of the computer; 4 The plug on the wall.

31

Line A leads to the toy car.
Line B leads to the train.
Line C leads to the duck.

32

2	3	5	6	9	7	4	8	1
8	9	4	1	3	2	7	5	6
1	6	7	5	8	4	9	3	2
6	5	8	4	2	3	1	9	7
7	2	3	9	1	6	5	4	8
9	4	1	7	5	8	6	2	3
5	8	9	3	7	1	2	6	4
4	7	2	8	6	9	3	1	5
3	1	6	2	4	5	8	7	9

33

Numbers 3, 6, and 8.

34

■	2	8	1	2	■	1	9	9	■
■	1	■	■	0	■	2	■	■	0	■
2	2	■	1	0	1	0	1	■	1	2
1	0	1	1	■	2	■	1	1	8	8
2	■	4	4	9	4	4	0	0	■	8
■	■	8	1	1	6	7	4	■	■
2	■	3	9	9	6	0	0	1	■	1
4	3	5	5	■	3	■	1	0	4	4
2	3	■	5	9	9	7	0	■	2	8
■	3	■	0	■	2	■	■	4	■
■	3	9	9	8	■	1	9	9	0	■

35

The shaded animal is a dog. Moth G has the same pattern on its wings as the bark of the tree, so it will be camouflaged.

36

24. One square balances 10 circles and one star balances 14 circles.

37

Screwdriver—$2.50; hammer—$10.00; tape measure—$5.50; set square—$1.50.

38

2, 10, 3, 12, 4, 7, 11, 5, 9, 1, 6, 8.

39

Picture 1 is missing a nail in the fence. Picture 2 is missing a stone on the pavement. Picture 3 is missing a leaf. Picture 4 is missing a brick. Picture 5 is missing a spot on the dog. Picture 6 is missing a nut on the wheel. Picture 7 is missing a leg on the dog. Picture 8 is missing a shirt pocket.

40

3	6	8	1	■	4	2	5	7
0	■	2	4	6	1	7	■	9
4	■	5	0	1	0	9	■	8
9	8	■	3	8	6	■	1	7
■	■	8	1	2	3	4	■	■
7	0	■	1	4	7	■	3	5
5	■	9	8	9	3	6	■	3
0	■	1	9	2	8	2	■	2
2	2	4	0	■	9	3	6	6

41

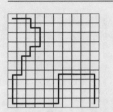

42

43

Silhouette 1 is picture f, and silhouette 2 is picture i.

44

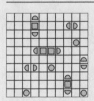

45

Picture "a" has an extra diamond on the sword. Picture "b" has an extra link in the chainmail. Picture "c" has an extra band on the sword handle. Picture "d" has an extra strap on the sandal.

46

1 and 4; 2 and 7; 5 and 8; 6 and 9. The odd one out is 3.

47

The shapes can be found:
in the kite, the roof of the house, the bird's tail-feather, the grassy area in front of the houses.

48

4	6	1	7	5	2	8	9	3
5	8	2	4	9	3	6	1	7
7	9	3	8	6	1	4	5	2
6	3	4	5	2	8	9	7	1
2	1	7	9	4	6	5	3	8
9	5	8	1	3	7	2	4	6
3	2	5	6	7	4	1	8	9
8	4	6	3	1	9	7	2	5
1	7	9	2	8	5	3	6	4

49

24. One star balances 6 circles and one square balances 4 circles.

50

Third block on top row, first and third block on fourth row.

51

FIRST NAME	SURNAME	YEAR DIED	CONVICTION
FRANZ	MULLER	1864	HAT
FREDERICK	FIELD	1936	CONFESSION
HERBERT	ARMSTRONG	1922	POISON
HORACE	MANTON	1947	SPELLING
JOHN	HAIG	1949	GALLSTONE

52

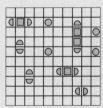

53

Cup 4.

54

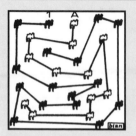

55

28. One square balances 12 circles and one star balances 2 circles.

56

Snapshot number 2.

57

58

Box number 4.

59

The matching halves are A and 4, B and 5, C and 8, D and 7, E and 1, F and 3, G and 2, H and 6.

60

Numbers 3 and 5.

61

The fish that has a seahorse on the left and a jellyfish on the right.

62

1 Flying Fortresses
2 Madame Poll's Parrots
3 Fred the Fire-Eater
4 Señor Pedro's Poodles
5 Clever Clowns
6 Agilles Acrobats
7 Crazy Carvellos
8 Jim the Juggler

63

Owls 4 and 6.

64

65

5. One square balances one star and four circles balance one star.

66

67

Number 1.

68

The man bought scarf e.

69

9	3	1	8	5	6	7	4	2
2	8	7	3	4	9	6	5	1
6	4	5	7	2	1	9	8	3
4	7	2	9	6	5	3	1	8
1	9	8	4	3	2	5	7	6
5	6	3	1	7	8	4	2	9
8	1	4	5	9	3	2	6	7
3	5	6	2	1	7	8	9	4
7	2	9	6	8	4	1	3	5

70

60 circles.

71

Peter—3, Rick; Alan—1, John;
Lex—2, Ian; Dave—4, Fred.

72

73

Amy—6; Belinda—1; Cathy—4.

74

The combination is 1781786.

75

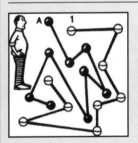

76

The man chose briefcase e.

77

The combination is 2031908.

78

The missing items are: the pillow, the
goldfish bowl, the doll, the model ship,
the clock, and the shelf. The damaged
item is the guitar, which has a broken
string.

79

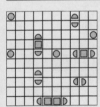

80

F-A-C-D-B-E.

7	5	8	1	6	2	3	4	9
6	2	9	5	3	4	8	7	1
1	4	3	9	8	7	5	6	2
5	9	4	8	2	3	6	1	7
2	8	7	6	1	9	4	5	3
3	1	6	4	7	5	2	9	8
8	7	1	2	4	6	9	3	5
4	3	5	7	9	8	1	2	6
9	6	2	3	5	1	7	8	4

82

Alicia, number 3; Bernadette, number 8; Claudia, number 6.

83

4	+	9	=	13
x		–		+
3	x	2	=	6
=		=		=
12	+	7	=	19

19	+	35	=	54
–		÷		÷
8	–	5	=	3
=		=		=
11	+	7	=	18

84

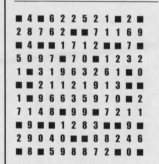

```
■ 4 ■ 6 2 2 5 2 1 ■ 2 ■
2 8 7 6 2 ■ ■ 7 1 1 6 9
■ 4 ■ 1 7 1 2 ■ ■ 2 ■
5 0 9 7 ■ 7 0 ■ 1 2 3 2
1 ■ 3 1 9 6 3 2 6 1 ■ 0
■ ■ 2 1 1 2 1 9 1 3 ■ ■
1 ■ 9 6 6 3 5 9 7 0 ■ 2
7 1 4 8 ■ 9 9 ■ 7 2 1 1
■ 9 ■ ■ 1 2 8 3 ■ ■ 9 ■
2 9 0 4 0 ■ ■ 8 8 2 4 6
■ 8 ■ 5 9 8 8 7 2 ■ 0 ■
```

The combination is 21121913.

85

86

Weights 1 and 4 will fall, and weights 2 and 3 will rise.

87

The treasure is buried in B5.

88

Number 3.

89

```
8 1 1 0 1   9   9   2 3 5 0 9
6   3   9   2 3 9 1 6   1   8
0   8   3   1   2   3   3   1
6   0   4 1 0   1   3   2   0
5 0 2 6 4   8 3 5   1 7 9 7 4
        0       2       0   0
2 4 4 1 5   9 1 5 0 5   9
3   3 9 2 6 4   6   3 8 1
8 1 0 8 7 1   6   3 0 4
  9   9 5 1 3 2 6   2
9 2 3 1 6   1 8 2   1 7 6 0 8
0   3   8 9 7 3   0
8 7 5 5 2   0   4   2 8 3 9 8
0   5 6 0   5 6 5   0
4 7 0 2 8   7 6 3   4 7 1 1 9
```

90

Number 4.

91

A1 and C2, B1 and A7, F1 and D7, G1 and D2, A2 and A5, C4 and E7.

92

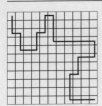

93

```
1 1 ■ ■ 1 ■ 1 ■ ■ 4 4
3 2 2 2 6 ■ 2 0 0 4 8
■ 5 ■ ■ 9 1 1 ■ ■ 5 ■
4 2 4 2 ■ ■ ■ 3 5 0 4
4 ■ 1 5 6 7 5 0 4 ■ 4
5 ■ 4 1 2 1 8 5 7 ■ 5
0 ■ 4 9 5 0 6 2 5 ■ 0
5 2 5 5 ■ ■ 2 1 2 1
■ 5 ■ ■ 1 2 2 ■ ■ 2 ■
5 0 6 2 5 ■ 4 0 4 2 1
2 4 ■ ■ 0 ■ 0 ■ ■ 5 5
```

The combination is 4121857.

94

Pot number 5. The bottom pot in each column has a lid like the top pot and a label like the middle one.

95

96

The missing number is 4. In each tile, the lower figure is obtained by multiplying the two digits of the upper number.

97

A and 7, B and 8, C and 9, D and 1, E and 3, F and 4, G and 2, H and 6, I and 5.

98

E inner is given as 4, so C inner, which must be an even number (clue 4) cannot be 4 or 8. If it were 2 and D inner 1, from clue 2, B outer and H inner would both be 3 and, from clue 3, the inner 6 could only be in segment G. C outer would therefore also be 6 as would F middle (clue 4). In that case F outer would have to be 12, which is impossible. So C inner must be 6 and D inner 3 (clue 4). So, from clue 2, B outer must be 7, H middle 8, and H inner 7, and since those two H numbers add up to 15, H outer must be 0. With the inner 6 being in C, the outer 6 must be in G (clue 3) and B inner must therefore be 5 (clue 2). To complete the B quota, B middle must be 3. We know D inner is 3, and, since, from clue 4, D outer is double D middle, those

numbers must be 8 and 4 respectively. F outer must be four times G middle (clue 4) and since the outer circle already has an 8, F outer must be 4, G middle 1, and F middle, from the same clue, 2. To complete their quotas, F inner must be 9 and G inner 8. C outer must be 2 (clue 4) and C middle 7. All inner numbers have now been inserted except in A, which is an odd number (clue 2), so it must be 1. To make up A's quota, the remaining odd numbers must be 5 and 9 and from clue 1, the 9 must be A outer and 5 A middle. Therefore E outer must also be 5 (clue 4) and E middle 6.
In summary:

Numbers given as outer, middle, inner.
A, 9, 5, 1.
B, 7, 3, 5.
C, 2, 7, 6.
D, 8, 4, 3.
E, 5, 6, 4.
F, 4, 2, 9.
G, 6, 1, 8.
H, 0, 8, 7.

99

Same palette and same picture—3, 5; same palette and different picture—1, 6; different palette and same picture—2, 4.

100

4. A sister and her brother, both married. One has a son and the other has a daughter.

101

102

Simply turn the bottle upside down and pour wine from another bottle into the recessed dimple and drink it. You have kept your word by "drinking wine from the bottle!"

103

The man chose T-shirt i.

104

105

Tex – 1, Jake; Ian – 4, Fred; Ken – 2, Joe; John – 3, Steve.

106

8, 3, 10, 2, 7, 1, 11, 4, 9, 6, 5.

107

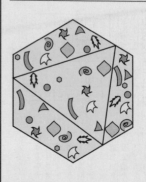

108

	Table 1	Table 2	Table 3	Table 4
N	Harry	Babs	Tessa (dummy)	Fred
E	Susie (dummy)	Kate	Connie	Lola
S	Jane	Roger (dummy)	Dot	Gordon
W	Peter	Alan	Michael	Eddie (dummy)
Contact	2 Diamonds	4 Spades	1 Heart	3 Clubs

109

Number 8.

110

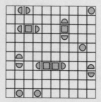

111

9	7	2	8	5	1	4	3	6
5	8	3	4	6	9	1	2	7
4	6	1	2	3	7	9	8	5
6	2	5	7	9	3	8	4	1
1	4	9	6	8	2	5	7	3
8	3	7	1	4	5	2	6	9
3	1	8	9	7	4	6	5	2
7	9	4	5	2	6	3	1	8
2	5	6	3	1	8	7	9	4

112

```
2 3 1 4 5 6     6 3 4 2 0 5
5       2 9 5 0 1 7       1
4 0 6 1 3 8     8 9 0 9 9   2
3   5   2   9 9 3   7   6   5
2   9   5       8   1   4 8 3
9 0 0 1 0 2   4 3 2 9 0 1   8
    8     8 8           3 0 8
  2   2   0   8 9 3 0 7 1
  4   3 7 1 9 2 4     1   5
3 1 8 8 6       2     3 9 9 2
    3     0   1 0 6 1 1 2     0
5 4 3 9 6     3 0       4 3 7 6
2     8     5   3 5 5 8       8
1 0 3 1   8 0 1     7       1 1 9
5       4     8   3 5 6 0       9
```

113

28. Circle = 3, diamond = 6, star = 5, and triangle = 4.

114

115

NAME	JOB	SUBJECT	PASSES
HUGH	POLICE	BRICKS	5
IVOR	POST	POETRY	3
WATT	SHOP	GRIBBLE	2
WENDY	BAR	SOAPS	4

116

A=6, B=4, C=5, D=8, E=7, F=3, G=2, H=1.

117

Mike – 2, Joan; Rex – 1, Mia;
Tom – 4, Jane; Ian – 3, Kate.

118

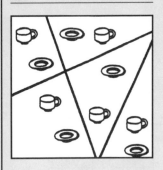

119

```
■ 4 ■ ■ 1 3 9 5 ■ ■ 1 ■
8 0 8 5 ■ 3 9 ■ 1 6 6 1
8 ■ 1 ■ 1 3 9 8 ■ 2 ■ 7
8 0 8 5 0 ■ ■ 1 3 9 5 7
5 ■ 7 8 9 4 3 2 2 5 ■ 7
■ ■ 1 4 1 0 1 6 4 4 ■ ■
1 ■ 6 3 8 7 2 0 6 4 ■ 7
9 2 0 5 5 ■ ■ 5 0 5 0 9
9 ■ 0 ■ 6 3 8 7 ■ 1 ■ 9
8 5 0 4 ■ 3 0 ■ 1 5 1 2
■ 2 ■ ■ 1 6 0 0 ■ ■ 0 ■
```

The combination is 14101644.

120

A – 10, B – 4, C – 6.

121

1 – B, 2 – C, 3 – A.

122

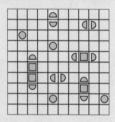

123

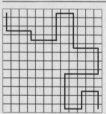

124

6	0	3	8	4	5		7	4	5	7	2	3
1			2	8	9	4	6		0			9
2	8	8	0	1	6		5	6	8	3	3	0
3		9		8		1	9	3		1		8	0
4		9		6			8		1		9	2	9
9	5	3	3	4	1		5	1	2	6	3	0	6
		6			8		8				7	3	4
	2		2		8		1	4	5	6	3	7
	9		8	5	0	3	3	7		5		8
7	2	3	5	3			8		6	8	3	9
	8			6		5	5	3	6	8	1	0
4	0	6	6	5		7		2		7	4	4	3
9			7			8		1	0	6	4		0
9	3	8	9		8	1	7		3		5	5	6
2			9			3		2	5	8	6		0

125

Triple 18; Double 9; Single 11.

126

Joe – 4, Jim; Fred – 2, David;
Ian – 3, Kyle; Mick – 1, Jack.

127

27.

128

Insects g, d, and o are shown in
silhouettes 1, 2, and 3, respectively.

129

130

Weights B and C will rise; weights A
and D will fall.

131

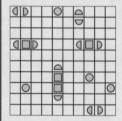

132

```
7 3 6 ■ 8 7 6 ■ 2 5 2
9 ■ 9 6 ■ 9 ■ 3 5 0 ■
9 ■ 5 ■ 7 8 6 ■ 1 7 7
4 1 0 ■ 9 ■ 2 5 3 7 8
■ ■ 3 3 6 3 9 3 ■ ■ 9
1 ■ 2 7 2 1 9 3 3 ■ 2
8 ■ ■ 9 9 8 0 0 1 ■ ■
9 4 1 8 2 ■ 8 ■ 2 8 1
8 8 5 ■ 5 4 1 ■ 7 ■ 9
■ 7 5 6 ■ 2 ■ 7 2 ■ 1
3 9 9 ■ 3 0 1 ■ 8 9 4
```

The combination is 2721933.

133

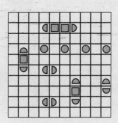

134

A and D are the pair; in B, the design on the cap is different and in C, the wheel is missing.

135

```
7 6 2 3   9 1 3 6 9   2 0 3 1
0     0   0       1 9       5
0     3 3 9 0 6   7 0 8 3 5 7
8 0 5 9       9 7 4         4
  4 3 2 8   2       6 3 1 2
3 8 0       8 3 3 0 7   9     5
  1 8 1 0       5 3 6 4     0
9 1 3       3 1 0 1 1     9   5
  8 2 7 1 4       2 1 0 9 5 4
  2     3 6 0 6 1 0       3
  4     5       5       6 3 0 9
4 4 8 1 5     2 7 3 0 5       5
1     6 6 3 0 2   2   2 0 8 5
0     7       2   9 4       0
8 7 9 0   6 8 4 1 1   8 3 3 5
```

136

Plug c is connected to the shaver.

137

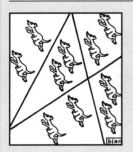

138

Photograph 8 is the one taken of the model.

139

Number 2.

140

The ball between the book and the teddy bear, underneath the pencil.

141

1F–5G, 2A–3E, 4A–6F, 3C–4D, 5C–9F, and 1A–9B.

142

Cup – $1.20; tube of toothpaste – $2.50; towel – $2.00; bar of soap – 50 cents.

143

4 and 5.

144

Number 4. In each row, the small rectangle makes a quarter-turn clockwise and the circle moves half as much as that in a counterclockwise direction.

145

1 The model's left hand is out of alignment with her arm; 2 The top of the yacht in the picture; 3 The edge of the frame of the right-hand picture is missing; 4 The artist's smock is uneven at the back; 5 The tube of paint has two tops; 6 The paint-box base is longer than its lid; 7 The model's left foot; 8 The wall-floor division is too high (between the model's calves); 9 One of the paint-brushes is outside the jar; 10 The table has only two legs.

146

Fork, candy, and box.

147

The details missing are: a) Button on shirt, b) Handle on bag, c) Label on washing machine, d) Collar on man's shirt, e) Drop of water, f) Part of screwdriver, g) Clothespin on line, h) Button on overalls.

148

Here's one possible solution.

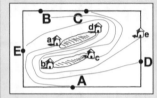

149

1 The flap on the left-hand porter's clothing; 2 The top leaf on the left-hand plant; 3 The woman's right foot; 4 The bow on the package.

150

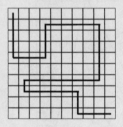

151

1 Damien, 2 Arthur, 3 Colin, 4 Errol, 5 Ben.

152

1 Window of spaceship; 2 Alien's antenna; 3 Bottom rung of ladder; 4 Door of spaceship.

153

7	6	3	9	8	5	4	1	2
2	5	8	1	7	4	9	3	6
9	1	4	6	2	3	8	5	7
4	3	2	5	1	6	7	9	8
8	9	5	2	4	7	1	6	3
1	7	6	8	3	9	5	2	4
3	8	1	7	5	2	6	4	9
5	2	9	4	6	8	3	7	1
6	4	7	3	9	1	2	8	5

154

The identical carts are 2 and 6.

155

The green mailbox cannot belong to number 228 or number 234 (clue 1), and the one at number 232 is blue (clue 4), so the green one must be at number 230. Arlene cannot live at 228 (clue 2), and, since her box is yellow (clue 2), this rules out numbers 230 and 232, so her home must be number 234. Now, by elimination, Mrs. Baron's red mailbox (clue 3) must be at number 228. So, from clue 1, Mrs. Gerber must live at number 232, and Gemma must be Mrs. Baron at number 228. Arlene is not Mrs. Fishbein (clue 2), so she must be Mrs. Flint, leaving Mrs. Fishbein at number 230. From clue 4, Louise is not Mrs. Gerber, so she must be Mrs. Fishbein, leaving Mrs. Gerber as Kate.

In summary:
228, Gemma Baron, red.
230, Louise Fishbein, green.
232, Kate Gerber, blue.
234, Arlene Flint, yellow.

156

First, Golden Goose, Ava Nother, Railway Approach. Second, Red Lion, Jean-Ann Tonic, Waterworks Alley. Third, Black Bull, Toby Jugge, Mill Street. Fourth, White Horse, Ivor Goodale, Factory Road. Fifth, Green Dragon, Phil Emupp, Gasworks Lane.

157

158

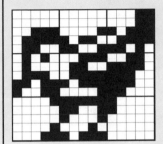

159

Vases 2, 6, and 11 are identical.

160

Rosalind painted in oils (clue 2), so the watercolor painting of the windmill, which was not by Nadine (clue 3), must have been done by Josephine, leaving Nadine as the artist who used pen and ink. So she did not draw the pond (clue 4), and must have depicted the village church, so she is Ms. Frame (clue 1). By elimination, Rosalind's oil painting must be of the pond. Her surname is not Canvass (clue 2), so it must be Pallett, leaving Canvass as the surname of Josephine.

In summary:
Josephine Canvass, windmill, watercolor.
Nadine Frame, village church, pen and ink.
Rosalind Pallett, pond, oils.

161

162

483

163

Earth, Jupiter, Pluto, Venus, Mercury, Saturn, Uranus, Mars.

164

165

Gretchen, who is six, cannot be number 4 (clue 1), and number 3 is seven (clue 4). Number 1 is a boy (clue 3), so, by elimination, Gretchen must be number 2. So, from clue 1, the child aged seven in position 3 is the cowherd's child. Maria, whose father is an apothecary (clue 5), cannot be number 1 (clue 3), so she must be number 4, and, from clue 5, she is five, leaving the boy in position 1 as eight. So he is not Hans (clue 2),

and must be Johann, leaving Hans as the seven-year-old son of the cowherd. From clue 3, Gretchen's father cannot be the butcher, so he must be the woodcutter, leaving Johann as the butcher's son.
In summary:
1, Johann, 8, butcher.
2, Gretchen, 6, woodcutter.
3, Hans, 7, cowherd.
4, Maria, 5, apothecary.

166

The extra details are: 6 – shield; 8 – coat of arms; 10 – hilt. The missing details are: 2 – doorway; 3 – knee; 7 – ear; 12 – tail.

167

Johnny is number 3 (clue 3). Number 1 cannot be Darren Poole (clue 2), or Shaun (clue 1), so he must be Garry. So, from clue 4, boy number 2 must have green boots. Those of boy number 4 cannot be red (clue 1), or brown (clue 2), so they must be black. So, from clue 4, Johnny, in position 3, must be Waters. Shaun's surname is not Brook (clue 1), so it must be Burne, leaving Garry's as Brook. So Shaun is not in position 2 (clue 3), and must be boy 4, wearing

the black boots. By elimination, this leaves boy 2, in the green boots, as Darren Poole. So, from clue 2, the brown boots must belong to the lad in position 1, Garry, leaving Johnny Waters wearing the red boots.
In summary:
1, Garry Brook, brown.
2, Darren Poole, green.
3, Johnny Waters, red.
4, Shaun Burne, black.

168

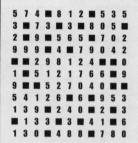

The combination is 5121766.

169

1 Paintbrush on floor, 2 Bird's tail, 3 Pane in skylight, 4 Palette, 5 Bird's wing, 6 Tube of paint on floor, 7 Artist's necktie, 8 Picture on floor.

170

171

The $5,000 prize cannot have been in box 1 or 6 (clue 7) or 2, from which Lynne got a smaller sum (clue 2), or 3 (clue 7 again) or 5 (clue 3), so must have been in box 4. From clue 7, a man opened box 3 and a woman box 5, and since no two men opened adjacent boxes, the remaining two females, Sharon and Susan, must have opened boxes 4 and 5. From clue 6, it was Susan who opened the winner's box 4, while Rob opened box 3, Sharon box 5, and, by elimination, Jim box 1. Both Lynne and Sharon won cash (clue 2), so, from clue 5, the box with the spoon was opened by either Michael or Rob. But, from clue 4, neither Michael nor Jim can have found the soap, so Rob must have done so, leaving Michael with the spoon and Jim with some cash. Therefore, from clue 5, Sharon must have won

$1,000. Now, from clue 4, Susan was the fifth contestant, and from clue 6, Rob was the sixth. The first contestant wasn't Jim (clue 1), or Lynne (clue 2), or Michael (clue 3), so must have been Sharon. From clues 2 and 3, either Michael or Lynne must have opened third or fourth, so Jim must have been second. He didn't collect 50 cents (clue 5), so Lynne must have done so, leaving Jim with $100, Michael as the third contestant (clue 3), and Lynne as the fourth. In summary:
1, second, Jim, $100.
2, fourth, Lynne, 50 cents.
3, sixth, Rob, bar of soap.
4, fifth, Susan, $5,000.
5, first, Sharon, $1,000.
6, third, Michael, wooden spoon.

172

2	1	2	■	2	2	4	■	4	1	5
5	■	2	9	■	8	■	1	3	2	■
6	■	6	■	6	3	4	■	2	4	2
4	2	9	■	5	■	1	1	0	1	9
■	■	8	1	7	6	6	8	■	■	6
8	■	1	9	4	1	9	5	1	■	0
4	■	■	8	0	9	2	1	3	■	■
5	9	3	1	9	■	1	■	7	4	1
5	8	8	■	6	1	4	■	5	■	0
■	8	2	4	■	1	■	1	3	■	1
5	2	8	■	8	0	4	■	6	5	7

The combination is 1941951.

173

The mirror image pairs are: 1 and 6, 2 and 7, 4 and 9, 5 and 8. Figure 3 is the odd one out.

174

Envelope – 20 cents; glue – 80 cents; pencil – 40 cents; roll of tape – $1.20.

175

Karen is studying law (clue 2), and Shuffell is studying medicine (clue 4), so Amanda Hart, whose subject is not theology (clue 3), must be majoring in engineering, and is therefore sitting North (clue 1). So, from clue 3, the theology student is in the East seat. We now know Ruff's subject is not engineering or medicine, nor is Ruff the surname of Karen, the law student (clue 2), so it must be the surname of the theology student in the East seat, which leaves Karen's surname as Diamond. From clue 2, her seat is West, which leaves Shuffell in the South seat. This person is not Petra (clue 4), so she must be Josephine, leaving Petra as Ruff.

North, Amanda Hart, engineering.
East, Petra Ruff, theology.
South, Josephine Shuffell, medicine.
West, Karen Diamond, law.

176

4	3	7	1	2	6	5	9	8
9	1	2	5	7	8	4	3	6
6	5	8	9	4	3	2	7	1
8	9	1	2	6	7	3	4	5
7	2	6	3	5	4	1	8	9
3	4	5	8	1	9	7	6	2
1	7	4	6	8	2	9	5	3
5	6	3	4	9	1	8	2	7
2	8	9	7	3	5	6	1	4

177

178

5 is the innermost number on strap D (clue 4), so that cannot be the strap referred to in clue 5, nor can strap E

(clue 3), or strap C (clue 7), while the outermost numbers on both straps A and F must be single-digit numbers (clue 2), so the strap referred to in clue 5 must be strap B. Clue 8 tells us the 17 is not the innermost number, so, from clue 5, the strap B numbers, reading outwards, must be 12, 1 and 17. So, from clue 8, the innermost number of strap E must be 18, and that on strap F therefore 8. We have now placed four innermost numbers, which total 43, so, from clue 1, the other two must total 21. From numbers already placed, we know these cannot be 18 and 3, 17 and 4, 16 and 5, 13 and 8, or 12 and 9, and clue 6 rules out both 15 and 6 and 11 and 10, so they must be 14 and 7. So, from clue 4, the 7 must be on strap C, and the 14 on strap A. We now know the single-digit number in the middle of strap A (clue 2) is not 1, 5, 7, or 8, nor, since the 15 is not an innermost number, can it be 6 (clue 6). It clearly cannot be 2 (clue 2). If it were 3 or 4, then, from clue 2, one of the other two numbers referred to would have to be 1, but we have already placed that number elsewhere, so, by elimination, it must be 9. We know the number outside it is not 7 or 8, nor, since we have placed 7 and 8, can it be 1 or 2 (clue 2). We also know that it is not 5, and, since we have placed the 5, it cannot be 4 (clue 2), so it must be 3

or 6, and so must the outermost number of strap F (clue 2). But we have placed the only even number on strap F (clue 3), so its outermost number must be 3, and the 6 must be on strap A. We know the 15 is not on strap B, so, from clue 6, it must be the middle number on strap F. Clue 6 now reveals the 10 as an outermost number. The middle number next to it is 16 (clue 6), so they cannot be on strap E, which already has one even number (clue 3), or on C, which has only one two-digit number (clue 7), so they must be on strap D. Since the 2 is not on strap C (clue 7), it must be one of the two even numbers on strap E (clue 3), which leaves the 4 on strap C. Clue 7 also places the 13 on strap C, leaving the 11 on strap E. From clue 3, the 2 must be the outermost number of strap E, and the 13 therefore is the outermost on strap C (clue 7), leaving the 11 and the 4 as the central numbers on their respective straps.
In summary:
(Reading outward)
Strap A: 14, 9, 6.
Strap B: 12, 1, 17.
Strap C: 7, 4, 13.
Strap D: 5, 16, 10.
Strap E: 18, 11, 2.
Strap F: 8, 15, 3.

179

Seven of Diamonds.
The hands are:
Straight Flush: 8D, 9D, 10D, JD, QD.
Four of a Kind: KC, KD, KH, KS and 10S.
Straight: 6S, 7C, 8H, 9S, 10C.
Flush: AH, QH, JH, 7H, 6H.
Full House: AC, AD, AS, 9C, 9H.
Two Pair: QC, QS, JC, JS, 7S.
Two Pair: 6C, 6D, 8C, 8S, 10H.

180

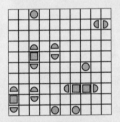

181

The objects appear in boxes A5, D5, E3, and G5.

182

Player 3 is bareheaded (clue 2). Player 1, whose surname is Green, is not James, in the floppy sunhat (clue 4), and it is Jacks who has the straw boater (clue 1), so Green must be wearing the baseball cap. Jacks cannot be number 4 (clue 1), and his headgear rules him out as number 3. We know he is not number 1, so he must be number 2, and, from clue 1, Charles must be the bareheaded number 3. By elimination, James must be player number 4. Jacks is not Walter (clue 3), so he must be Donald, leaving Green as Walter. Charles is not Byass (clue 2), so he must be Wood, leaving Byass as James.
1, Walter Green, baseball cap.
2, Donald Jacks, straw boater.
3, Charles Wood, bareheaded.
4, James Byass, floppy sunhat.

183

184

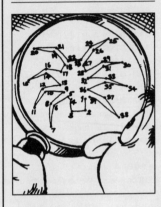

185

From the top: C, E, D, B, A, F.

186

187

The identical twins are C and F.

188

The heart is not the 8 or the jack (clue 1), and the 5 was a club (clue 3), so the heart must have been the 2. So it was not dealt by Charlie (clue 4), or Bevis (clue 1), and Dean's card was a diamond (clue 2), so it must have been Andrew who dealt the heart. Therefore it cannot have been card 1 or card 2 (clue 5), and clue 1 rules it out as card 4, so it must have been card 3. So, from clue 1, card 4 must be the 8, and, from clue 5, card 1 must be the jack. We now know the 5 of clubs is not any of cards 1, 3, or 4, so it must be card 2. So, from clue 3, the spade, which we know is not card 3, must be card 4, and it is therefore the 8. Now, by elimination, Dean's diamond must be the jack in position 1, and, from clue 4, Charlie must have dealt the 8 of spades, leaving Bevis as the dealer of card 2, the 5 of clubs.
1, Dean, jack of diamonds.
2, Bevis, 5 of clubs.
3, Andrew, 2 of hearts.
4, Charlie, 8 of spades.

189

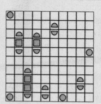

190

The painting is number 2 and side C should be at the top.

191

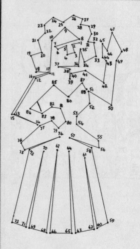

192

The objects appear in squares b6, d4, d6, and g4.

193

Plug C.

194

The man with the beard bought a fez. The young man wearing a T-shirt bought a backpack. The woman wearing the triangle-patterned dress bought a flower hair decoration. The woman with the circular belt buckle bought a jacket. The man wearing glasses bought a book. The fair-haired young man in the foreground bought a sweater. The woman wearing the polka-dot dress bought a necklace. The man with the dark wavy hair replaced his tie with a new bowtie. The man in overalls replaced his shirt with a new T-shirt. The fair-haired man in the turtleneck sweater bought a baseball cap.

195

196

8	2	6	5	1	7	9	3	4
5	3	1	8	4	9	7	2	6
7	9	4	6	3	2	1	5	8
3	6	8	4	7	5	2	9	1
2	1	7	3	9	8	6	4	5
9	4	5	2	6	1	3	8	7
6	5	3	1	2	4	8	7	9
4	7	2	9	8	6	5	1	3
1	8	9	7	5	3	4	6	2

197

A	B	C		
	A	B	C	
C		B		A
	A		C	B
B	C		A	

198

4	5	2	6	1	3
2	3	4	5	6	1
5	6	1	2	3	4
3	2	5	1	4	6
6	1	3	4	2	5
1	4	6	3	5	2

199

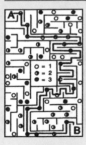

200

1 There are two moons; 2 Right-hand sleeve of nightgown missing; 3 Door of right-hand trailer not in line; 4 Square wheel on car; 5 Steering-wheel in the middle of the car.

201

The boy in the red sweater was not Danny or Lewis, who had the chocolate bar (clue 4), and Kevin's sweater was blue (clue 1), so the red sweater must have been Simon's. The first friend met did not have the red sweater (clue 4), or the blue one (clue 1), and number 3 wore the beige sweater (clue 2), so number 1 must have been in the green one. So, from clue 3, it was boy 2 who was eating a banana. We know his sweater was not beige or green, and he was not Simon, in the red sweater (clue 3), so he must have worn the blue sweater, and is therefore Kevin. So, from clue 1, boy 1, in the green sweater, was eating a lollipop. This rules out Kevin, Lewis, and Simon, so he must have been Danny. By elimination, Simon must have been eating an apple, and Lewis must have been the third friend Tommy met, wearing the beige sweater, which leaves Simon as friend number 4.

In summary:
1, Danny, green, lollipop.
2, Kevin, blue, banana.
3, Lewis, beige, chocolate bar.
4, Simon, red, apple.

202

C	A	D	E	B
A	B	E	D	C
B	D	A	C	E
E	C	B	A	D
D	E	C	B	A

203

11.

204

The third from the left in the second row down and the second and fourth from the left in the third row down.

205

489

206

First, beach, 25 minutes, bottle top. Second, park, 15 minutes, spoon. Third, farmer's field, 40 minutes, toy car. Fourth, own garden, 35 minutes, wrench. Fifth, friend's garden, 20 minutes, doorknob.

207

The values of the shapes are: circle=1, star=5, square=2. So the first column adds up to 16.

208

209

210

211

The fourth one down in the left-hand column, the bottom one in the middle column, and the middle one in the right-hand column.

212

213

Tangles 2 and 4 will knot.

214

215

216

217

218

1. Kate, 2. Brother, 3. Sally and Andrew,
4. Cousin, 5. Great-grandson, 6. Four, 7.
Simon and Bella.

219

Dr. Adam – 4, Ian; Dr. Felp – 2, Mike;
Dr. Carn – 1, John; Dr. Stern – 3, Joe.

220

```
4 1 8 9 2    2   2   9 3 7 2 1
3   1   3    5 2 0 4 9   5   6
9   5   7    3   2   2   8   9
1   5   7 0 5   9   0   8   9
4 1 6 3 6    8 1 4   6 2 2 5 9
    5        3       3 4
7 1 7 0 3    5 0 3 2 6   1
4     1 4 2 6 8   7   9 5 0
8 4 1 0 2 3       4     6 2 5
  0      7 6 4 1 3 2   0
6 2 0 0 8    5 1 3   8 1 6 5 5
1     3    9 8 8   3       9
5 0 3 7 1    1   2   8 9 0 9 3
0     9 7 4   6 8 6       2
5 1 1 6 9    4 5 1   3 9 0 9 2
```

221

From the top: A, B, C, D, E, F.

222

Pen – $3.75; pencil – 89 cents;
ruler – $1.20; bottle of ink – $3.95.

223

Monday, plumber, "Hello," "Buzz off!"
Tuesday, aunt, "Who's a pretty boy?"
"Get lost!"
Wednesday, TV repairman, "Good
morning," "Beat it!".
Thursday, carpenter, "Nice to meet
you," "Get out of here!"
Friday, sister, "How do you do?" "Go
away!"

224

225

226

A		B		C
	C	A		B
B			C	A
C	B		A	
	A	C	B	

227

N	F	Y	K	C
Q	J	W	H	T
G	U	R	B	M
A	L	D	V	O
X	P	I	S	E

228

Numbers 3, 6, 8, and 10.

229

The Falldownlaughing show liked the
video of Trev's little sister falling out of
bed best!

230

6	6	4	4	4	3	6	6
5	0	1	2	5	4	0	2
0	0	3	4	5	2	5	0
1	5	1	1	1	2	5	2
1	4	3	0	6	1	4	3
2	5	5	2	2	3	3	1
6	6	0	3	4	0	6	3

231

Weights A and B will rise, and weights C and D will fall.

232

Plug B should be inserted in the socket.

233

Vases e and k are identical.

234

From clue 5, the 1 cannot be in column 1 or column 5, and, since there are no two-digit numbers in columns 1 or 4 (clue 1), the 1 cannot be in column 2 or column 3 (clue 5), so it must be in column 4. But it cannot be in B4 (clue 6), so it must be in D4. So, from clue 5, the 12 must be in C5, and the 10 in E3. The 8 is directly above the 13 (clue 7). This cannot be in column 1 or column 4 (clue 1), nor, since the 13 cannot be in square D2 (clue 1), can they be in column 2 either. Nor can the number 13 be in E5 (clue 4), which rules out column 5. Therefore, from clue 7, the 8 must be in A3, and the 13 in C3. So, from clue 4, square E5 must contain the 7. The 11 cannot be in column 1 or column 4 (clue 1), nor can it be in

square A5 (clue 1), so it must be in column 2. But it cannot be in D2 (clue 1), so it must be in B2. The 9 is not in a corner square (clue 2), which leaves only squares B4, C1, or D2. But it cannot be in B4 or D2 (clue 6), so it must be in C1. Since the 6 is directly below the 2 (clue 3), it cannot be in D2, B4, A1, or A5, so it must be in E1. The 2 is therefore in A1 (clue 3). The remaining numbers to be placed are 3, 4, and 5. So, from clue 6, the 5 must be in B4 and the 3 in D2, which leaves the 4 in A5.

In summary:

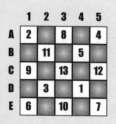

235

Tulip, A – 4; basket, B – 6; shield, F – 1; ice-cream cone, G – 3.

236

237

Fragments 1 and 3 complete wheel A.

238

239

The man bought suitcase g.

240

The 19 in B3 is row 3's only two-digit number (clue 2), so the 9 cannot be in any of rows 1, 3, or 4 (clue 3). The only single-digit number in row 2 is the 7 (clue 2), so the 9 must be in row 5, but not in square E5 (clue 3). Since the 11 is in row 4 (clue 6), clue 5 rules out the 16 for A4, so the 9 cannot be in A5. Nor can it be in C5 (clue 8). Since the 17 is in column D (clue 7), clue 5 rules out the 12 for E5, so, from clue 3, the 9 cannot be in D5 and, by elimination, must be in square B5. Therefore, from clue 3, the 16 must be in B4, and the 12 in C5.

There must be exactly one zero in each row and each column (clue 1). We know the one in row 5 is not in B5 or C5, nor can it be in D5 (clue 7), or E5 (clue 5), so it must be in A5. The 1 in row 5 (clue 9) cannot be in E5, since the 6 is in row 1 (clues 5 and 9), so, by elimination, it must be in D5. The 17 in column D cannot be in D1 or D4 (clue 7), and clue 2 rules out D3. Therefore it must be in D2, and D1 therefore contains a zero (clue 7). The zero in row 3 cannot be in A3, C3, or D3 (clue 1), and we know it is not in B3, so it must be in E3. Clue 1 now rules out A4, D4, and E4 for the zero in row 4, which therefore must be in C4. The one in column B cannot be in B1 (clue 1), so it must be in B2. Clue 6 now places the 11 in E4, and the 5 in D4, so, from clue 7, the 8 must be in D3. The number in E5 cannot be any of 16 to 20 (clue 5), and we know it is not any of 1, 5, 6 (clue 9), 7 (clue 2), 8, 9, 11, or 12, so it must be one of 2, 3, 4, 10, 13, 14, or 15. Clue 5 rules out 3, 4, and 14, since we have placed 8, 9, and 19, and also rules out 2, 10, or 13, since we know none of 1, 9, or 12 is in C2, so, by elimination, 15 must be in E5, and, from clue 5, 20 must be in A4, and 14 in C2. Since the numbers in column E total 45 (clue 4), those in E1 and E2 must total 19. Therefore, since we have placed the 12, the 7 cannot be in E2, and

therefore must be in A2 (clue 2). Now, from clue 4, the 13 must be in E2, so, from that clue, E1 must contain the 6. The 3 cannot be in C3 (clue 8), so, from clue 10, it must be in A3, and the 10 in A1. The 18 is not in C1 or C3 (clue 8), so it must be in B1. Clue 6 now places the 2 in C1, and the 4 in C3.

In summary:

	A	B	C	D	E
1	10	18	2	0	6
2	7	0	14	17	13
3	3	19	4	8	0
4	20	16	0	5	11
5	0	9	12	1	15

241

Picture a is missing a button on the jacket sleeve. Picture h is missing a rectangle on the label. Picture j is missing a tie. Picture k has part of the newspaper missing. Picture f has a dark hat band. Picture l has an extra hook. Picture b has an extra orange.

242

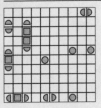

243

10	21	23	7	4
25	1	18	13	16
5	14	20	9	2
8	11	6	22	19
15	24	3	17	12

244

D	E	C	B	A
E	A	D	C	B
C	B	A	E	D
A	C	B	D	E
B	D	E	A	C

245

$9 \times 8 - 7 \div 5 + 1 \div 7 \times 3 = 6$.

246

1 Castle's turret; 2 Arrow; 3 Bush under tree; 4 Patch on trousers; 5 Feather in cap; 6 Mountain on the left; 7 Castle's entrance; 8 Boy's arm.

247

Susan's surname is Niven (clue 4) and Knight is the quiz show host (clue 2), so Laura the news anchor (clue 3) must be Robins, and Knight's first name must be Donna. By elimination, Susan Niven must be the current affairs host. She didn't train to be a nurse (clue 4) or a teacher (clue 5), so must have trained as a lawyer. Donna Knight didn't train to be a teacher (clue 1), so must have trained as a nurse, leaving news anchor Laura Robins as the former student teacher.

In summary:
Donna Knight, quiz show host, nurse.
Laura Robins, news anchor, teacher.
Susan Niven, current affairs host, lawyer.

248

249

2	6	9	3	5	1	7	8	4
4	5	7	9	8	6	1	3	2
8	1	3	2	7	4	6	5	9
9	8	2	7	6	3	5	4	1
5	3	6	4	1	2	8	9	7
7	4	1	8	9	5	2	6	3
3	9	5	6	2	7	4	1	8
1	7	4	5	3	8	9	2	6
6	2	8	1	4	9	3	7	5

250

251

Pieces 2 and 3 are part of the main picture.

252

From the top: C, E, A, D, B, F.

253

254

C1 and A4.

255

24.

256

B	D	C	A	E
E	A	D	C	B
A	C	E	B	D
D	B	A	E	C
C	E	B	D	A

257

A2 and D4.

258

Vases 4, 5, 7, and 11.

259

1	6	4	3	5	7	2	8	9
2	8	3	4	9	6	1	7	5
5	7	9	2	1	8	4	3	6
3	5	6	1	7	2	9	4	8
9	2	1	5	8	4	7	6	3
8	4	7	9	6	3	5	2	1
7	1	8	6	4	9	3	5	2
4	3	5	8	2	1	6	9	7
6	9	2	7	3	5	8	1	4

260

The four objects are in squares 4B, 4E, 7B, and 6D.

261

1	3	6	2	4	0	5	6
5	2	0	2	1	1	0	2
4	4	0	2	4	6	0	3
5	0	6	5	6	3	5	5
2	3	0	4	1	4	5	0
1	6	6	6	2	1	3	1
1	2	3	4	4	5	3	3

262

2	3	7	1	6
9	1	9	4	9
9	8	5	9	6
2	4	0	6	9
9	7	3	3	6

263

	C	A		B
A		B	C	
B	A	C		
	B		A	C
C			B	A

264

265

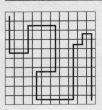

266

Since the figure 5 is not printed in brown (clue 1), the brown stamp must be the 10 cents value. This cannot be stamp 4 (clue 2), so that stamp, which has a 1 in its value panel (clue 3), must be the 15 cents value. So, from clue 4, stamp 2 must be blue. Clue 2 now tells us the cathedral design, which has a zero in its value, cannot be stamp 4, so it must be stamp 2, and, from that clue, stamp 1 must be the brown 10 cents value. The same clue reveals the value of the blue stamp 2 as 50 cents. Now, by elimination, stamp 3 must be the 25 cents value. The mountains are not the design on the 10 cents stamp in position 1 (clue 5), and the same clue tells us they cannot be on the 25 cents value, since we know the 50 cents stamp is blue. We know they are not on the 50 cents value either, so they must be the design on the 15 cents stamp, number 4. Therefore, from clue 5, the red is the 25 cents stamp, leaving the 15 cents value as the green stamp. Clue 3 tells us stamp 3 does not depict the harbor, so its subject must be the waterfall, leaving the harbor as the design on stamp 1, the brown 10 cents value.

In summary:
1, harbor, 10 cents, brown.
2, cathedral, 50 cents, blue.
3, waterfall, 25 cents, red.
4, mountains, 15 cents, green.

267

268

B		A	C	
	C	B		A
A		C		B
C	B		A	
	A		B	C

269

Piece number 2.

270

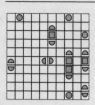

271

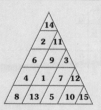

272

2	6	1	4	4	3	0	3
2	3	5	5	6	6	4	2
0	1	0	2	1	1	1	4
5	3	0	0	5	3	0	5
0	6	1	2	1	6	4	1
4	3	3	4	0	5	5	6
2	4	6	3	2	2	6	5

273

Benedict Marshall,
announcer, 8 years.
Denzil Banks, baggage
handler, 6 years.
Lawrence Adamson,
traffic controller, 7 years.
Matthew Ledger, security
guard, 4 years.
Quentin Forrest,
electrician,
5 years.

274

275

Tom has a violin, Dick a trumpet, and
Harry a drum.

276

A3 and D3.

277

278

9:00, Roland Brake, hill start, Church Hill.
9:30, Helen Weales, reversing, Balmoral Circle.
10:30, Rex Chance, parking, Mill Road.
11:00, Ron Gear, emergency stop, Hawthorn Way.
11:30, Vera Swerve, signaling, Market Street.

279

280

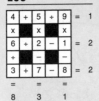

281

1 Vase handle, 2 Flower stem, 3 Castle tower, 4 Dog's leg, 5 Man's tie.

282

Rope 4.

283

Weights 1, 2, and 5 go up, and weights 3 and 4 go down.

284

	1	2	3	4
A	8	2	11	4
B	3	12	5	7
C	6	10	1	9

The 12 is in square B2 (clue 1). Since neither the 2 nor the 1 is in column 1 (clue 5), neither can be one of the factors of 12 referred to in clue 1. Nor is the 4 in column 1 (clue 4), so the two numbers in question must be 3 and 6. Since the 6 is next to the 10 in the same horizontal row (clue 2), it cannot be in B1, so, from clue 1, the 6 must be in C1, and the 10 in C2 (clue 2), while, from clue 1, the 3 must be in B1, and, from clue 2, the 8 must be in A1. We have placed the 3 and the 10, so, from clue 3, the number in C3 cannot be 2 or 3, nor can it be 4 (clue 4), so, since the highest number in the layout is 12, from clue 3, the 1 must be in C3, and the 9 therefore in C4. Clue 4 now places the 7 in B4, the 4 in A4, and the 5 in B3. Clue 5 therefore tells us the 2 is in A2, and the 11 in A3.

285

1 Leaf in the top left-hand corner;
2 Lower window;
3 Circle on the bag; 4 Right-hand root;
5 Pocket; 6 Doctor's mirror; 7 Shrub to the right; 8 Lapel.

286

The blue box contains 58 items (clue 2), and the green box contains the screws (clue 3), so the 43 nails, which are not in the brown box (clue 1), must be in the red one. We know the green box does not contain 43 or 58 items, and clue 3 rules out 65, so it must contain 39 screws. So, by elimination, the contents of the brown box must be 65 items. These are not washers (clue 3), so they must be carpet tacks, and they are in box C (clue 4), which leaves the blue box containing 58 washers. The green box cannot be box D (clue 3), since it has two neighbors, so that clue places it as box B, and the blue box containing the washers must be box A (also clue 3), leaving the red box as box D.
In summary:
A, blue, 58 washers.
B, green, 39 screws.
C, brown, 65 carpet tacks.
D, red, 43 nails.

287

The clocks add on an hour and ten minutes each time, so the final clock will show the time as 12:30.

288

1	6	3	6	0	6	0	2
6	2	2	6	6	5	3	1
2	4	1	2	4	4	0	0
0	5	5	3	0	4	5	3
4	1	3	1	4	5	3	3
1	5	0	0	1	6	4	2
6	2	3	2	1	4	5	5

289

This puzzle does not need any solution.

290

Hose B.

291

Number 3 with side b at the top.

292

293

From the top: B, C, D, A, E, F.

294

The children have the following number of candies: David=15, Tony=14, Sally=8, Simon=7, Katie=4, Philip=2. Altogether the children have 50 candies.

295

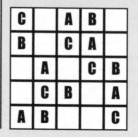

296

297

The four snapshots taken at the same time are: top row, first and fourth; and bottom row, second and third.

298

299

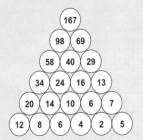

1	2	4	5	2	3	2	3
1	5	6	4	4	2	3	1
1	4	2	2	1	0	3	4
2	5	1	6	5	6	3	3
3	5	4	6	6	2	5	1
0	5	3	6	4	6	1	0
0	4	5	0	6	0	0	0

300

```
            167
        98      69
     58     40      29
  34     24     16     13
20    14    10     6      7
12    8     6     4     2     5
```

301

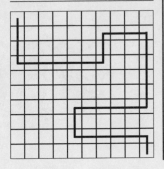

302

303

```
    5 1 0   1 7 9     4 7 4 8 0 3 8
  2   7   8   3         2   1         0
  5 3 6 0 3 0 1       3 4 0 5 2       1
  1   3     3   1         3       4 2 1
  6 9 0 9     4 5 0 1 0 3     3       3
  0   8       8 8 2       8 2 4 9 1   6
  1       1     5     3 7 7 2     4   6
      3 0 9 9 1 0           6   3
      6   2       2     1 3 8 5 0 0   2
  6 1 1 6 8 3       0           6     3
  0       5           1 2 5     4 2 1 6 6
  5 8 4     2         2     7     8   5
  5   5 9 9 1 2 6       7 1 3     5   2
  4 2 0     8       9 5 0 1       5 0 5 5
  4   6 1 5 1 9         8   6
```

304

Pictures 2 and 3 are the same. Picture 1 has a pebble missing in the bottom right-hand corner. Picture 4 has an extra window in the sandcastle.

305

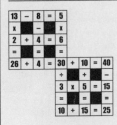

13	−	8	=	5				
x		−		x				
2	+	4	=	6				
=		=		=				
26	+	4	=	30	+	10	=	40
		÷				+		−
		3	x	5	=	15		
		=		=		=		
		10	+	15	=	25		

306

D	A	C	E	B
E	C	B	D	A
A	B	D	C	E
C	E	A	B	D
B	D	E	A	C

307

1	2	4	5	1	1	1	3
6	2	2	5	6	2	5	3
2	1	2	5	6	3	6	3
2	6	4	5	0	4	0	4
0	3	0	5	6	0	0	0
5	3	6	5	4	4	6	3
3	1	4	1	4	0	1	2

308

Josie's pet is a puppy (clue 5). Julie's cannot be a canary (clue 4), or a tortoise (clue 3), so it must be a cat. So she is not the girl in position 4, who has a canary (clue 5). This fact also rules out Josie as girl 4, and clue 1 rules out Jenny, so it must be Jemima who is in position 4. By elimination, the tortoise must belong to Jenny. Since Jemima is in position 4, Julie cannot be in position 3 (clue 3). Nor can she be in position 2 (clue 4), so she must be in position 1. So, since Julie's pet is the cat, Josie cannot be in position 2 (clue 2). Therefore she must be in position 3, and position 2 must be occupied by Jenny. Clue 5 now tells us Josie is ten. Julie cannot be eight (clue 4), or nine (clue 3), so she must be eleven. Jenny cannot be nine (clue 1), so she must be eight, leaving Jemima as the girl aged nine.

In summary:

1, Julie, 11, cat.
2, Jenny, 8, tortoise.
3, Josie, 10, puppy.
4, Jemima, 9, canary.

309

Wire A leads to the hovercraft, wire B leads to the boat, wire C leads to the car.

310

Tangles B and D will knot.

311

312

From left to right: 9, 3, 4, and 11.

313

9	4	1	2	6	5	3	8	7
6	5	8	7	3	9	4	1	2
7	2	3	8	4	1	6	5	9
8	9	4	3	5	6	2	7	1
3	7	2	9	1	8	5	4	6
1	6	5	4	2	7	9	3	8
5	1	7	6	9	3	8	2	4
2	8	6	5	7	4	1	9	3
4	3	9	1	8	2	7	6	5

314

315

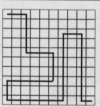

316

Plug c is connected to the toothbrush.

317

318

	C	B		A
A			C	B
B		A		C
	A	C	B	
C	B		A	

319

Tony is flying kite B. Jo is flying kite C. Pete is flying kite A.

320

D	B			A	C
C	A	D	B		
B		A	D	C	
A	C			B	D
	D	C	A		B
		B	C	D	A

321

From the top: D, A, E, B, C, F.

322

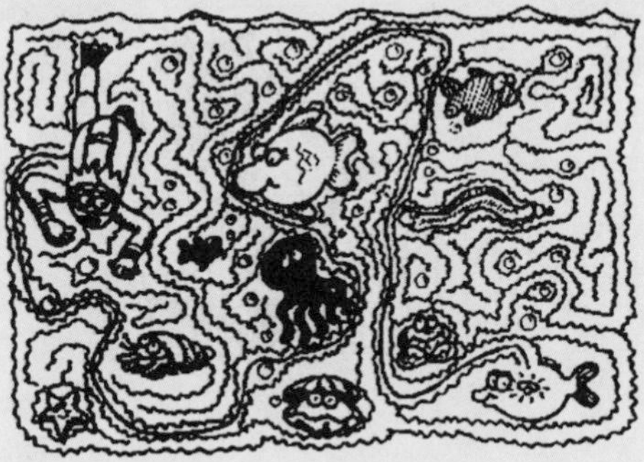

323

Cube number 2.

324

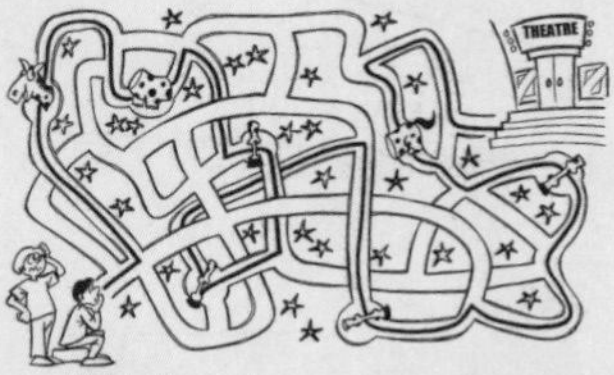

325

Across: spade + club = 15 (row 4), so diamond = 7 (row 1); thus heart = 4 (row 2), spade = 8 (row 3), and club = 7 (row 4).
Down: heart + diamond = 25 (column 1), so club = 15 (column 3); thus spade = 12 (column 4), diamond = 15 (column 2), and heart = 10 (column 1).

326

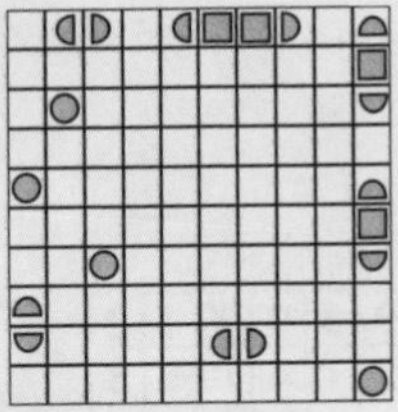

327

3	+	8	–	5	=	6
x		–		x		
4	+	6	÷	2	=	5
–		+		–		
9	–	1	–	7	=	1
=		=		=		
3		2		3		

328

Letter number 4.

329

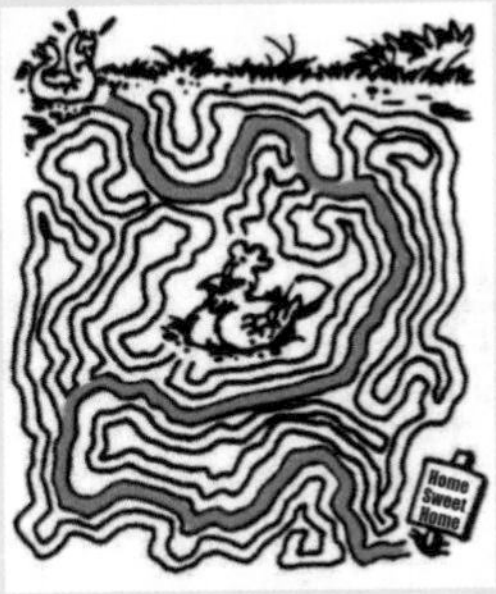

330

Numbers 4 and 6.

331

3	8	4	9	5	6	7	1	2
1	6	9	2	7	4	8	5	3
7	2	5	3	1	8	6	9	4
4	3	1	7	2	9	5	6	8
9	5	8	1	6	3	2	4	7
6	7	2	4	8	5	9	3	1
8	9	7	6	3	1	4	2	5
5	4	3	8	9	2	1	7	6
2	1	6	5	4	7	3	8	9

332

Triangle, ladder, butterfly.

333

Pyramid 1.

334

335

336

The twins are A and C. In B a bolt is missing from the table leg, and in D the chef has hair.

337

338

5	1	4	9	3	6	8	7	2
3	8	7	4	2	1	9	5	6
2	9	6	5	8	7	3	1	4
7	5	1	6	4	3	2	8	9
6	2	9	1	5	8	7	4	3
8	4	3	2	7	9	5	6	1
1	6	5	8	9	2	4	3	7
9	7	8	3	6	4	1	2	5
4	3	2	7	1	5	6	9	8

339

	A		C	B
C		B	A	
A	B	C		
	C		B	A
B		A		C

340

341

From the top: F, D, B, C, A, E.

342

Paul Hand was Esther's partner (clue 4), so Martina must have been partnered by Richard. So he held the ace of hearts (clue 2). Therefore, from clue 1, Ruff had the ace of diamonds in the North hand. We now know Paul Hand did not have the aces of diamonds or hearts, and it was a woman who was in the West seat with the ace of spades (clue 3), so Paul must have had the ace of clubs. So he was not South (clue 5). We know he was not North, and he cannot have been West (clue 3), so he must have been East, and Esther was therefore West, who had the ace of spades (clues 3 and 4). By elimination, Richard, who we know was not North, must have been South, and Ruff, in the North seat, was therefore Martina. Esther's surname is not Tenace (clue 3), so it must be Trick, leaving Tenace as Richard.

In summary:
North, Martina Ruff, ace of diamonds.
East, Paul Hand, ace of clubs.
South, Richard Tenace, ace of hearts.
West, Esther Trick, ace of spades.

343

B	C	A		
		B	A	C
	A	C		B
C			B	A
A	B		C	

344

345

Go from 1 to: 6 – 3 – 8 – 7 – 5 – 6 – 8 – 5 – 6.

346

Fragments 1 and 4 complete wheel A, and 2 and 3 complete wheel B.

347

The man in seat 13 of row A (clue 6) cannot be Peter or Henry (clue 1), or Robert (clue 4). Judy cannot have a seat numbered 13 (clue 5), so that clue rules out seat 13 in row A for both Charles and Vincent, so, by elimination, the man in that seat must be Tony. Angela is also in row A (clue 1), which must also seat one more woman (clue 3). This is not Nina, who has seat 12 in row B (clue 2), and it cannot be Janet or Lydia (clue 7). Clue 5 rules out Judy, so, by elimination, Maxine must have a front row seat. This cannot be numbered 10 or 11 (clue 4), and we know it is not 13, so it must be 12. Therefore Robert has seat 10 in that row (clue 4), which leaves Angela in seat 11. So, from clue 1, Peter has seat 11 in row B. There must be a second man in that row (clue 3). This is not Henry, who must be in row C (clue 1), and clue 5 rules out Vincent for either seat 10 or seat 13 in that row, which are the only two still vacant. We know Tony and Robert are in row A, so, by elimination, Charles must be in row B. He cannot be in seat 13 (clue 5), so he must be in seat 10. Therefore, from clue 5, Judy must be in seat 10 of row C, and Vincent in seat 11 of that row. So, from clues 1 and 7, Henry must have seat 12 of row C, and Lydia seat 13 of the

same row, leaving seat 13 in row B
occupied by Janet.

In summary:
Row A: 10, Robert; 11, Angela; 12,
Maxine; 13, Tony.
Row B: 10, Charles; 11, Peter; 12, Nina;
13, Janet.
Row C: 10, Judy; 11, Vincent; 12,
Henry; 13, Lydia.

348

End number 4.

349

Tangles 1 and 3 will knot, but 2 and 4
won't.

350

A		B		C	D
	C	D		A	B
D	A		B		C
	B	C	A	D	
C			D	B	A
B	D	A	C		

351

352

John – 4, Joan; Fred – 3, Jane;
Mike – 2, Mia; Liam – 1, Kate.

353

4	1	1	5	5	5	2	3
1	1	2	6	0	6	6	3
6	4	6	5	0	2	5	6
4	0	3	3	0	5	2	1
6	2	6	4	3	0	2	1
2	4	4	4	1	2	4	5
3	5	0	1	3	0	3	0

354

4	9	4	9	3	5
8	9	5	2	6	7
5	1	8	1	5	2
8	6	6	9	8	4
1	7	2	3	6	3
3	4	2	7	7	1

355

B	C	E	A	D
D	A	B	E	C
E	D	A	C	B
C	E	D	B	A
A	B	C	D	E

356

		C	B	A	
A	C	B			
B			A	C	
	A		C	B	
C	B	A			

357

4	2	7	8	9	4		2	3	7	8	1	0	
3		7	3	6	0	6		9					5
9	3	3	3	2	1		5	0	0	2	1		9
0		0		8		5	9	8		2		3	0
1	1		0				0		9		8	1	3
3	8	2	4		1	2		5	5	2	6	0	0
		8			3		0				2	3	7
	1		4		9		1	8	3	1	3	4	
	1		6	3	5	0	8	1			2		5
8	1	8	3	4			2			7	9	1	0
	8			0		8	0	8	3	3	4		0
4	8	2	9	8		2		4			6	3	6	2
0		3			6		7	2	9	0			3
1	3	9	0		6	1	2			3		7	0	6
4		6			0		1	2	4	3			6

358

Mitzi—B, Fritzy—C, Bitzy—A.

359

Path C.

360

D	B			A	C
C	A	D	B		
B		A	D	C	
A	C			B	D
	D	C	A		B
		B	C	D	A

361

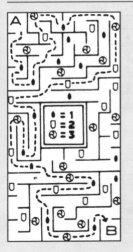

● = 1
▯ = 2
⊕ = 3

362

Number 2.

363

1—E, 2—D, 3—A, 4—B, 5—C.

364

365

7	3	9	2	8	1	4	6	5
8	2	4	6	7	5	1	9	3
6	1	5	9	3	4	7	2	8
3	4	7	5	2	9	8	1	6
9	8	6	4	1	7	3	5	2
2	5	1	8	6	3	9	7	4
5	7	8	1	4	6	2	3	9
4	6	3	7	9	2	5	8	1
1	9	2	3	5	8	6	4	7

366

D	A	C	E	B
E	C	B	D	A
A	B	D	C	E
C	E	A	B	D
B	D	E	A	C

367

368

		C	B	A
A	C	B		
B			A	C
	A		C	B
C	B	A		

369

The pairs are 1 and 6, 2 and 9, 3 and 8, and 4 and 7. The odd girl out is number 5.

370

The five fakes are: the picture of the house, where the gatepost is too tall; the picture of the clown, where the decoration on his hat is too high; the picture of the horse and cart, where the cart's side is too low; the picture of the seagull, where the gull's right wing is too low; and the picture of the ballerina, where part of her skirt is missing.

371

5	8	9	1	3	7	6	4	2
6	1	7	9	2	4	3	8	5
3	2	4	8	5	6	7	1	9
2	7	8	4	6	1	5	9	3
9	4	6	5	7	3	8	2	1
1	5	3	2	9	8	4	7	6
4	6	5	7	1	2	9	3	8
7	9	2	3	8	5	1	6	4
8	3	1	6	4	9	2	5	7

372

Impression 4 was made by the stamp.

373

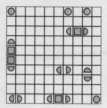

374

Letter 5.

375

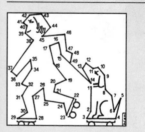

376

Number 2.

377

C	D	E	B	A
B	E	A	D	C
E	A	D	C	B
D	B	C	A	E
A	C	B	E	D

378

9	8	2	1	6	4	5	3	7
1	3	4	9	7	5	8	6	2
6	5	7	2	3	8	1	9	4
7	4	3	8	2	6	9	1	5
2	9	6	3	5	1	7	4	8
8	1	5	4	9	7	3	2	6
5	7	1	6	4	9	2	8	3
3	6	9	5	8	2	4	7	1
4	2	8	7	1	3	6	5	9

379

Route D will get the lifeguard to Freddie.

380

B	A	E	C	D
E	C	A	D	B
D	E	C	B	A
C	B	D	A	E
A	D	B	E	C

381

C			A	B
	B	C		A
A		B	C	
B	C	A		
	A	B	C	

382

```
■ 1 1 9 7 1 5 ■ 2 1 1 6 6 8 9
3 ■ 2 ■ 0 ■ 6 ■ ■ 2 ■ 1 ■ ■ 3
3 4 2 8 7 2 9 ■ 4 3 1 4 8 ■ 0
7 ■ 5 ■ 6 ■ 8 ■ ■ 3 ■ 4 9 8 1
5 2 5 9 ■ 8 5 1 7 0 ■ ■ 7 ■ 2
9 ■ 2 ■ 4 0 7 ■ ■ 6 4 6 3 0 3
4 ■ ■ 1 ■ 2 ■ 2 3 7 5 ■ 1 ■ 1
■ 9 7 8 5 2 2 ■ ■ ■ 5 ■ 3 ■ ■
■ 1 ■ 2 ■ 0 ■ 1 6 9 4 4 5 9 ■
2 8 0 6 4 8 ■ 9 ■ ■ 5 ■ ■ 1 ■
2 ■ ■ 0 ■ ■ 3 3 1 ■ 4 2 3 2 5
5 2 3 ■ 4 ■ ■ 2 ■ 1 ■ 4 ■ ■ 6 ■
4 ■ 4 4 5 7 1 7 ■ 6 5 8 ■ 6 ■
6 6 9 ■ 8 ■ 7 7 0 4 ■ 8 8 1 7
3 ■ 8 5 2 3 9 ■ ■ 6 ■ 7 ■ ■ ■
```

383

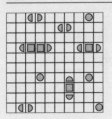

C	F	A	B	D
B	D	E	C	A
E	A	B	D	C
D	B	C	A	E
A	C	D	E	B

384

9, 2, 14, 4, 10, 1, 12, 3, 6, 11, 5, 7, 13, 8.

385

386

A Trish and Zoe; B Ros and Viv;
C Una and Xena; D Sue and Wendy.

387

Jim has bought picture C, and side
number 4 should be at the top.

388

Tex – 3, Jane; Chip – 1, Hazel; Ty – 4,
Kate; Jed – 2, Jo.

389

The missing piece is number 6.

390

391

From the top: 6 – 5; 9 – 10; 3 – 4;
2 – 1; 8 – 7.

392

393

1 – F; 2 – C; 3 – H; 4 – A; 5 – G;
6 – D; 7 – B; 8 – E.

394

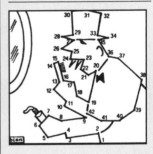

395

A		B		C	D
	C	D		A	B
D	A		B		C
	B	C	A	D	
C			D	B	A
B	D	A	C		

396

397

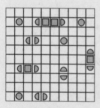

398

The identical pictures are B and E.

399

```
1 0 2 6 4    1    3    7 1 6 0 5
3   1    1   5 1 3 0 0    0    7
9   1    0   8      3 0 0   7 7 1
5   9    8 7 2    0   9 9   7 3
6 3 0 4 4    8 4 9   8 1 4 6 4
      2          2        0   8
2 3 1 0 4      7 3 9 3 0    1
6   0 8 8 9 2 1   9    2 3 3
9 1 3 3 4 5      2    8 3 0
   8      5 2 3 4 8 1    1
2 6 8 6 6    3 1 2    4 1 5 4 4
4       2    6 1    0 3    4 3
5 1 9 0 0    6 0    7 0 2 2 2
2     5 5 0    1 8 3        6
6 3 7 1 5    7 0 6    8 1 9 9 5
```

400

401

A	B	E	C	D
D	A	B	E	C
C	D	A	B	E
E	C	D	A	B
B	E	C	D	A

402

Buffalo.

403

	B	A		C
A	C		B	
	A	B	C	
B		C		A
C			A	B

404

John=Train, Joe=Ball, Sue=Doll.

405

Butterflies B and F are identical.

406

Poster A shows Jacob (clue 2) and poster D shows Churchman, so Herbert, who's shown on the poster horizontally adjacent to the one showing "Butch" McColl (clue 1), can't be shown on poster C, nor does poster C show Silvester Jaggard (clue 2), so it must show Matthew. We now know that Silvester Jaggard isn't shown on poster A, C, or D, so he must be on poster B. By elimination, Herbert must be on poster D, and, from clue 1, Matthew, on poster C, must be "Butch" McColl. By elimination, Jacob's surname must be Wolf. So, from clue 3, "Pony" must be Silvester Jaggard on poster B. Herbert Churchman on poster D isn't "Apache" (clue 4), so his nickname must be "Rio" and "Apache" must be Jacob Wolf on poster A.
In summary:
A, Jacob "Apache" Wolf.
B, Silvester "Pony" Jaggard.
C, Matthew "Butch" McColl.
D, Herbert "Rio" Churchman.

407

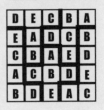

408

Teddy bears C and E.

409

410

411

From the top: B, A, C, D, E, F.

412

Monday, mopping, library, television.
Tuesday, polishing, shop, art class.
Wednesday, baking, friend, bingo.
Thursday, washing, sister, whist.
Friday, ironing, hairdresser, choir.

413

9	1	6	3	8	5	7	4	2
2	4	3	9	7	1	6	8	5
8	5	7	4	2	6	3	1	9
5	8	4	6	9	2	1	7	3
6	2	1	7	5	3	4	9	8
3	7	9	1	4	8	5	2	6
1	3	2	8	6	4	9	5	7
4	9	5	2	3	7	8	6	1
7	6	8	5	1	9	2	3	4

414

From the top: D, B, E, A, F, C.

415

8 stars and 10 tears.

416

Numbers 2, 4, 6, and 9.

417

Mr. Baker, Outlaw, whippet, scared of cats.
Mrs. Carrick, Flash, red setter, alcoholic.
Miss Flatman, Eddie, boxer, eats flowers.
Mr. McCrae, Tiffany, corgi, antisocial habits.
Ms. Scanlon, King, Dalmatian, chases policemen.

418

419

420

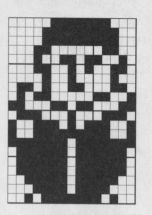

421

1	4	2	8	9	6	5	7	3
8	5	3	4	1	7	2	9	6
7	6	9	3	2	5	4	1	8
9	2	1	7	6	4	3	8	5
6	8	5	9	3	1	7	4	2
3	7	4	2	5	8	1	6	9
5	9	8	1	7	3	6	2	4
4	3	7	6	8	2	9	5	1
2	1	6	5	4	9	8	3	7

422

423

A	B	C		
		B	A	C
B	C	A		
	A		C	B
C			B	A

424

425

426

Building 1 dates from 1825 (clue 2). Building 3 was not built in 1761, nor is it the station, which dates from 1854 (clues 1 and 4), so it must have been built in 1772. So, from clue 3, building 1 is the windmill. Clue 4 now tells us the tollhouse dates from 1761, which leaves building 3 as the old inn. From clue 5, the Lewis family cannot live there, so their home must be in the old tollhouse dating from 1761. The Vickers family do not live in the windmill or the inn (clue 3), so their home must be the former station built in 1854. The Carters do not own the oldest building (clue 4), so they must own the windmill dating from 1825, leaving the Mortons at the inn built in 1772. So, from clue 1, the railway station must be in location 4, leaving building 2 as the old tollhouse.

1, windmill, 1825, Carter.
2, tollhouse, 1761, Lewis.
3, inn, 1772, Morton.
4, railway station, 1854, Vickers.

427

Number 1.

428

Box c is the same as the one being held by the magician.

429

430

First, Eric, chicken, lunch.
Second, Alan, pork, morning snack.
Third, Oswald, beef, light supper.
Fourth, Jasper, goose, afternoon snack. Fifth, Percival, turkey, evening banquet.